In Defense of Purity

Dietrich von Hildebrand

In Defense of Purity

An Analysis of the Catholic Ideals
of Purity and Virginity

Dietrich von Hildebrand

—

Foreword by Alice von Hildebrand

Preface by Leo Scheffczyk

HILDEBRAND
PROJECT

Originally published in German as *Reinheit und Jungfräulichkeit.*
KölnMünchenWien: Oratoriums Verlag, 1927.

First English Edition:
London: Sheed & Ward, 1931.

Published 2017 by Hildebrand Press
1235 University Blvd., Steubenville, Ohio 43952

Cataloguing-in-Publication Information
Von Hildebrand, Dietrich, 1889–1977, author.
[Reinheit und Jungfräulichkeit. English]
In defense of purity : an analysis of the Catholic
ideals of purity and virginity / Dietrich von Hildebrand
; foreword by Alice von Hildebrand
; preface by Leo Scheffczyk—Sixth edition.
pages cm
Includes index.
LCCN 2017942244
ISBN 978-1-939773-03-6

1. Sex—Religious aspects—Catholic Church.
2. Virginity—Religious aspects—Catholic Church.
I. Von Hildebrand, Alice, writer of foreword.
II. Scheffczyk, Leo, writer of preface. III. Translation
of: Von Hildebrand, Dietrich, 1889–1977.
Reinheit und Jungfräulichkeit. German. IV. Title.
BV4647.C5V62 2017 241'.66
QBI17-823

Book design by Mark McGarry, Texas Type & Book Works
Set in Adobe Caslon

Cover design by Marylouise McGraw

Cover Image: Portrait of a Young Woman, by Sandro Botticelli, in the Städel of
Frankfurt, Germany. Image from Wikimedia Commons.

Front Cover Font: Circular Bold by Lauren Brunner

www.hildebrandproject.org

Contents

Dietrich von Hildebrand

Dietrich von Hildebrand was born in Florence in 1889, and studied philosophy under Adolf Reinach, Max Scheler, and Edmund Husserl. He was received into the Catholic Church in 1914. He distinguished himself with many publications in moral philosophy, in social philosophy, in the philosophy of the interpersonal, and in aesthetics. He taught in Munich, Vienna, and New York. In the 1930s, he was one of the strongest voices in Europe against Nazism. He died in New Rochelle, New York in 1977.

Hildebrand Project

We advance the rich tradition of Christian personalism, especially as developed by Dietrich von Hildebrand and Karol Wojtyla (Pope St. John Paul II), in the service of intellectual and cultural renewal.

Our publications, academic programs, and public events introduce the great personalist thinkers and witnesses of the twentieth century. Animated by a heightened sense of the mystery and dignity of the human person, they developed a personalism that sheds new light on freedom and conscience, the religious transcendence of the person, the relationship between individual and community, the love between man and woman, and the life-giving power of beauty. We connect their vision of the human person with the great traditions of Western and Christian thought, and draw from their personalism in addressing the deepest needs and aspirations of our contemporaries. For more information, please visit: www.hildebrandproject.org

Editorial Board

Special Thanks

We gratefully acknowledge the vision and generosity of the many friends who have supported the publication of this book.

EXTRAORDINARY SUPPORT

The Catholic Association Foundation · Alice von Hildebrand · Robert L. Luddy · Patricia C. Lynch · James N. Perry, Jr.

PATRONS

Daniel and Teresa Cotter · Madeline L. Cottrell · Julia Harrison · Robert Kreppel · H. Kimberly Lukens · Charles A. Mastronardi Foundation · Jeffrey and Mary Petrino

BENEFACTORS

John F. Cannon · Rafael Madan and Lilian Casas Foundation · Allison Coates and Joshua Kneubuhl · Geoff and Lauren Gentile · Edward and

Alice Ann Grayson • Patrick J. Hart • Richard and Vera Hough • Timothy J. Joyce • John Kelly • Franco S. Madan • William and Robin Mureiko • Kevin and Dawn O'Scannlain • Martha Reichert • Stanley Stillman

FRIENDS

Rev. Ryan J. Adams • Tessa Breen • JA & A Brennan family, Australia • Andrew Cannon • Sheila A. Conforti • Andrea Corallo • John and Claire Foster • Fr. Andrew Fryml • Arthur and Mariluz Giron • Willard and Shirley Haley • Jo-Ann M. Henry • Roy and Elizabeth Heyne • John Iverson • Michael and Rebecca Matheson Miller • Scott McCawley • Gerard and Germana Mitchell • Roberta De Monticelli • Bartolomé Ribas Ozonas and Elisabeth Wannieck Sattler • Barbara Parrish • Britt and Noah Riner • Thomas W. Shaw • Stan Sienkiewicz • Rev. Robert F. Slesinski • Madeleine F. Stebbins • Martha A. Sullivan • Jon Tveit • Martín von Hildebrand • Katherine Weir • Fritz K. Wenisch • Kent and Nancy Young

Foreword
By Alice von Hildebrand

RARELY DOES a book come along that takes up a perennial theme in such a fresh and unexpected way as to transform all subsequent discussion of the issues. This is one of those books. A concern for purity, especially purity of heart, of course, is as old as many ancient faiths, and common to most. But in this book, Dietrich von Hildebrand inaugurated a new approach to thinking about sex and how the body reveals the human person.

Few thinkers have succeeded so well in showing that the intimate sphere is essentially *deep*; that it touches the very core of the human person in a way that other bodily desires, like hunger and thirst, do not. The human person is so closely united with his body that they essentially belong together. This uniquely close connection between sex and the person sheds light on why sexual vices are a sort of desecration that befoul the human soul in a way that gluttony and drunkenness do not.

Written to appear in this new edition of *In Defense of Purity*, by Dietrich von Hildebrand (Steubenville: Hildebrand Press, 2017).

From a young age, and continuing through his formative philosophical studies, Hildebrand was convinced that sex was different from other bodily instincts. He had an innately strong sense for the mysterious domain of sex, and was an attentive student especially of the affective aspects of the human person (see, for example, his other books *The Heart* and *The Nature of Love*).

Hildebrand's intuitions of the depth and mystery of sexuality fully blossomed in him when he entered the Catholic Church in 1914 at the age of twenty-four. He now saw more clearly that the intimate sphere was linked to God, and that in marriage man and woman collaborate with God in the bringing forth of a new human person. But he also saw that purity was opposed, so to speak, from two sides. On the one hand, there was the perennial allure of the flesh and the destruction left in its wake. On the other hand, in reading contemporary Catholic works following his conversion, he was struck by their emphasis on the dangers of *impurity* and that they seemed to forget that the ugliness and gravity of this sin could only be perceived in the light of the shining virtue of purity.

So this is what he set out to do in *In Defense of Purity*: to explore purity as a positive reality and only in light of its beauty to describe its contrary. (This is the same approach that Karol Wojtyla would later take to purity in his *Love and Responsibility*, which was the philosophical ground of his famous *Theology of the Body* talks). The book explores purity in connection both to married love and to consecrated virginity. To contemporary eyes and ears, this pairing will seem contradictory; in Hildebrand's treatment, however, we see how purity lies at the root both of a self-giving sexual love and also of the self-gift, soul and body, made by the consecrated virgin.

From its first appearance in 1927, *In Defense of Purity* was widely recognized as groundbreaking. This was not because its author proposed abandoning perennial Christian teaching on love and sexuality. On the contrary, he contributed by deepening the Christian understanding. He was the first Catholic thinker to distinguish the "procreative" meaning of the conjugal act, which had long been recognized, from the "unitive" meaning of it. This distinction has been crucial for all Christian reflection on marriage since. And, indeed, the Church has incorporated the "procreative" and "unitive" meanings of marriage into her teaching at the Second Vatican Council.[1]

The book is full of other rich insights, many of which my husband would go on to develop in later writings. Particularly significant is his idea that only love—and love as a movement of the heart and not just of the will—has the power to transform sexual passion into an unparalleled expression of love.

Another major contribution is his critique of the idea that purity is just a lack of bodily vitality or the absence of sexual desire. He opens our eyes to the fact that "insensuality" (his term for a weak sensibility for the vital sphere), far from being a virtue (even if, inevitably, it may prevent some people from committing sins of impurity) is in fact something most regrettable: for it cripples those affected by it from a full understanding of the nobility of a total self-donation. It is in giving oneself that one is fully oneself. This also sheds light on virginity, which, likewise, is not a holding back of oneself but a total, complete, heroic giving of oneself to God.

For nearly a century, In Defense of Purity has been pivotal in the lives of countless readers, some discovering the gift and meaning of their sexuality and others finding and feeling confirmed in a religious vocation. One such reader was Dorothy Day, who counted In Defense of Purity among the best books she had read on the Christian life. Its influence is clear in her own reflections on purity:

> Some choose evil because they have not seen the good...Those who suppress sex wrongfully, who hate the flesh, either become neurotic prudes or fall into the opposite extreme of excess. Those unwilling or unable to accept the attitudes of the conventional and puritanical bourgeoisie are easily betrayed by that "poisonous fascination" of which Dr. Von Hildebrand writes.[2]

1. See *Pastoral Constitution on the Church in the Modern World*—Gaudium et Spes, 1965, par. 50.
2. Dorothy Day, *On Pilgrimage* (Grand Rapids, MI: Eerdmans, 1999), 63.

No work that I am aware of offers a more fundamental and penetrating treatment of the great and beautiful and neglected virtue of purity. May it once again find a receptive audience.

Alice von Hildebrand
Widow of Dietrich von Hildebrand
Co-Founder, Hildebrand Project

Preface
By Leo Scheffczyk

In Defense of Purity is one of Dietrich von Hildebrand's smaller works, yet for this very reason it became a jewel in the hands of this master of thought and word. He has very nearly perfected the intellectual penetration and illuminating interpretation of an object made possible by the immediate philosophical intuition of essences. So vividly are the values of purity and virginity made to emerge from the heart of the Christian ethos, and to stand forth in their individual character, that they begin to shine on their own.

The inner tension and stirring quality of these subtle reflections derives neither from the moral requirements of purity and virginity nor from any pedagogical guidance for their realization. These would be derivative, secondary expressions of a more extrinsic approach to the topic.

What Hildebrand offers is this: by looking at these Christian attitudes through the lens of love, he achieves an intuition of their value and radiance that appeals immediately to the mind. But this does not come at the expense of the sphere of sensuality and the body. On the contrary:

This preface originally appeared in the German edition, St. Ottilien: EOS Verlag, 1981.

Hildebrand sees "purity" as the spiritual and personal transformation of sensuality, which ultimately contains a reflection of the divine. "Virginity" entails a further intensification of this value through a belonging to God in the totality of one's humanity and directly to Christ for the sake of the kingdom of God. If ever the dualism opposed to the Christian conception of the body has been rebutted and completely dispelled, then it is in this work in which Hildebrand bears eloquent witness to the spiritual character of the body in both marriage and virginity.

When this book first appeared in 1927, many people were brought to a new depth of understanding and some even to conversion. Times have changed so much that the entire realm of values has been reduced to the biological, and the Christian ethos to a form of moral self-improvement. All this only increases the significance of this work, which cuts through the fog of the zeitgeist and raises our eyes to the full mystery of creation, which is uniquely revealed in an appreciation of the bodily sphere.

Leo Scheffczyk[†]
Professor of Theology, University of Munich

Preface
By Dietrich von Hildebrand

THE FOLLOWING study is the result of lectures delivered at a session of the Federation of Catholic Students' Unions held at Innsbruck in 1925. Its purpose is an analysis of the nature of purity and virginity, not a study of sex education nor the formulation of practical rules of conduct, not even a defense of purity and virginity *against their detractors*. For this reason the question of which I shall primarily treat is not how much is lawful in this field, but what constitutes the complete virtue of purity and wherein the ideal of purity consists. It is my intention to undertake a detailed study of ethics in which the principles and facts on which my treatment of these particular problems is based will be fully explained. The reason for uniting in one study purity and virginity is of a practical nature. Although virginity represents in its significance and value something completely new and autonomous with respect to purity, its inmost nature is intelligible only when we have understood that of the person, which is also the decisive factor for purity.

I must express the deepest gratitude to my friend and loyal colleague S. J. Hamburger, for the liberal and most valuable help in the preparation of this book.

May this book assist many readers to attain a deeper understanding of the radiant virtue of purity and the mysterious beauty of virginity and inspire them with a new love for both so that more and more "they may be able to comprehend with all the saints, what is the breadth and length and height and depth" (of the Divine Love) "and to know the love of Christ which surpasses all knowledge."

Purity

CHAPTER ONE

Sex Distinguished from Other Bodily Appetites

IT IS IMPOSSIBLE to understand the virtue of human purity without first considering briefly the distinctive character and unique position of sex in human nature. Among the activities and appetites of the human body, sex occupies a unique position. When we consider eating, drinking, and sleep—indeed, bodily pleasure as a whole—we find this entire province of human experience characterized by a lack of depth. Delight in a good dinner, for example, or annoyance at a bad one, belongs of its nature to the superficial zone of human experience. The enjoyment of sleep, or the pleasure we take in being comfortable or in a glass of wine, is also essentially on the surface, and men who give experiences of this kind an important place in their lives we consider superficial.

Moreover, immoderate desire of such things is relatively superficial in its negative value. Excess in eating and drinking is no doubt a sin. Nevertheless, a Sancho Panza who gives free rein to his desire for food, drink, and sleep may be regarded as innocent by comparison with an avaricious, hard-hearted, or revengeful character. The satisfaction of these physical appetites acquires a somewhat deeper significance only when it is not the fulfillment of greedy desire, but a necessity of life in the most literal sense. The glass of water drained by the thirsty, the meal that restores strength to the hungry, the bed that welcomes the man exhausted by fatigue, are no longer the objects of innocent pleasure or of greed. They belong, on the contrary, to moments when man becomes conscious of his profound dependence and weakness, in which, beaten back to the frontier of bodily existence, he experiences these goods as his redemption from uttermost need. Then well-nigh inevitably he perceives them in their true character as gifts from God's hand. And the intensity of his need measures his experience of deliverance. We have but to think of the Lamentations of Jeremiah[1] to see displayed in a particularly clear and expressive form the depth of which even this sphere of bodily experience can be capable. And to the sphere of these profound bodily experiences also belong illness, acute physical suffering, and the release from these, for example, in convalescence.

The difference of quality within the bodily sphere between these latter experiences and the manifestations of desire, of which we first spoke, is obvious at first sight. The craving of the thirsty man for a drink of water has nothing of greed in it, nor yet of an innocent, good-natured animality; it is thoroughly noble and arouses nothing but pity and compassion, whereas greed in this department reveals at best a certain innocence and childish good nature, which evoke a smile.

Sex, on the other hand, as contrasted with the other departments of bodily experience, is *essentially* deep. Every manifestation of sex produces an effect which transcends the physical sphere and, in a fashion quite unlike the other bodily desires, involves the soul deeply in its passion. In its purely physiological aspect sexual experience possesses a distinctive quality totally unlike any other bodily pleasure, and the attraction exerted by the other appetites cannot be compared to the physiological attraction of sex. The positive and negative values attaching to sex belong to a level far deeper than those which attach to the other bodily appetites. Indeed, these sexual experiences are characterized by a specific character

---

1. "To their mothers they say: Where is corn and wine? When they swoon as the wounded in the streets of the city, when their soul is passed out into their mothers' bosom" (Lam. 2:12).

of mystery which, like the other essential elements of sexuality on which at present we can but briefly touch, must be reserved for fuller treatment later. In their distinctive quality there is something which penetrates to the very root of man's physical being, and which the other bodily experiences attain only when life itself is at stake. They have in them something extraordinary which exceeds the bounds of everyday life. They display a depth and a gravity which removes them altogether from the province of all other bodily experiences.

And, as a result, it is characteristic of sex that in virtue of its very significance and nature it tends to become incorporated with experiences of a higher order, purely psychological and spiritual. Nothing in the domain of sex is so self-contained as the other bodily experiences, for example, eating and drinking. The unique profundity of sex in the physical sphere is sufficiently shown by the simple fact that a man's attitude toward it is of incomparably greater moral significance than his attitude to the other bodily appetites. Surrender to sexual desire for its own sake defiles a man in a way that gluttony, for example, can never do. It wounds him to the core of his being, and he becomes in an absolutely different and novel fashion guilty of sin. And even as compared with many other domains of experience which are not physical, sex occupies a central position in the personality. It represents a factor in human nature which essentially seeks to play a decisive part in man's life. Sex can indeed keep silence, but when it speaks it is no mere *obiter dictum*, but a voice from the depths, the utterance of something central and of the utmost significance. In and with sex, man, in a special sense, gives himself.

This central position is determined by two factors. The first is that here body and soul meet in a unique fashion, a point to which we must return later. The second is the peculiar intimacy of sex. In a certain sense sex is the secret of the individual, which he instinctively hides from others. It is something which the person concerned feels to be altogether private, something which belongs to his inmost being. Every disclosure of sex is the revelation of something intimate and personal. It is the initiation of another into our secret. It is for this reason that the domain of sex is also the sphere of shame in its most characteristic sense. We are preeminently ashamed to unveil this secret to others. Whether a man is modest or immodest depends first and foremost on his attitude to sex.[2]

This intimate character is a further proof of the special depth of sex as contrasted with the other bodily functions. But before everything else it reveals the central position of sex. And because sex is the secret of the individual, to disclose and surrender it is in a unique sense to surrender oneself.

---

2. Our limits do not allow us to discuss the nature of modesty. We can touch only in passing on a problem whose profundity is for the most part inadequately recognized, and remark upon the great variety of forms into which shame can be divided. There is the shame which makes a man seek to hide any personal ugliness or deformity; for example, a hunchback. There is the shame which tries to conceal a fault, and so on. From shame of this more generic kind, whose characteristic expression is the fear of appearing ludicrous, we must distinguish the incomparably deeper and thoroughly noble shame which conceals something because it is particularly intimate; for example, when a man is ashamed to show his most delicate and deepest feelings to outsiders. The modesty which belongs to the domain of sex is therefore the most perfect example of shame, because in it privacy is the primary consideration. There could be no greater mistake than to explain the tendency to conceal sex as exclusively, or even primarily, an endeavor to hide something disgraceful and ugly. As compared with shame as the attitude of being ashamed with reference to others, modesty represents a novel factor. It is even more exclusively confined to the domain of sex. But it is grounded not only in the intimacy of sex, but in the intrinsic awe it inspires, awe of its extraordinary and mysterious quality, and more particularly an instinctive dislike of the impudent, the irreverent, the defiling, and the sinister as they are specifically bound up with its misuse. See further the discussion of purity in chapter 6.

CHAPTER TWO

The Relation of Sex to the Spiritual Life

IN VIRTUE OF its profound centrality and intimacy, as also of its mystery, sex is capable of a particular relationship with love, the most spiritual and the deepest of all experiences.

It is quite impossible to regard the union of love and sex in marriage as due exclusively to its aim of propagation. We should not forget that the Church assigns three ends to marriage, which St. Augustine sums up by the words *proles*, *fides*, *sacramentum*—offspring, fidelity, the sacrament. There exists, however, a profound relation of quality between the bodily union and that psychological and spiritual factor of specifically matrimonial love formulated under the terms *mutuum adjutorium* (mutual assistance) and *fides* (fidelity) as one of these three ends. We have here to do with an organic unity, deeply rooted in the attributes of wedded love on the one hand and of sex on the other. And just because sex is so uniquely intimate and represents the secret of the person concerned, the sexual gift of one person to another signifies an incomparably close union with that other and a self-surrender to him or her. The sexual union is thus the organic expression of wedded love, which intends precisely this mutual gift of self.

There are, to be sure, certain modern theories which exaggerate beyond all measure the part played by sex, while nevertheless missing its deeper significance, and venture the absurd thesis that love in general, and not only the love between man and woman, is a sublimation of the sex instinct. Such a doctrine betrays, in the first place, complete failure to understand the spiritual structure of the personality and, secondly, an entire misapprehension of the nature of love, the supreme actuation of the spirit.[1] We can understand the nature of love without any reference to sex; indeed, it is only in that way that we can understand clearly the distinctive quality of the genuine act of love. We can understand it best in its source, the Divine Love, as it issues from the most sacred Heart of Jesus, where every thought of sex fails. It is therefore of the first importance to realize the complete independence and sovereignty with respect to sex of love generally. But the specific quality not only of love as such, but of wedded love in particular, is independent of the physical aspect of sex. What distinguishes wedded love from other kinds of love — for example, love of parents or children or the love between two friends — is the quality of the love itself, the distinctive correlation between two persons, the completion of both parties, which only this kind of love affects, and that unique splendor which invests "being in love" in the noble sense. It is impossible to reduce all this to so-called sex instinct.

1. Sigmund Freud's thesis, on which the so-called psychoanalytic method is based, in spite of the valuable psychotherapeutic discoveries that it has produced, embodies a completely erroneous view of the structure of human personality, which betrays the influence of an exploded sensationalism. Its first radical error is that it regards the body and the physiological life as the "form" of the soul, not the spiritual soul as the "form" of life and the body. As sensationalism has always done, it constructs man from below, instead of recognizing in the spiritual center, made in the image of God, the formal actuating principle. A second error, equally fundamental, is the transformation of ultimate objective analogies between different spheres in the human person into real causal relations, as soon as sex is in any way concerned. As the sight of the bodily eye possesses a profound analogy with all forms of mental apperception in which the object faces me from a distance, and I enlighten it with the clear beam of the apperceiving consciousness, whereas the sense of touch with its immediate contact is the prototype of an entirely different group of mental relationships to an object — for instance, my becoming sensible of the benevolence and love; or, on the contrary, of the hatred and enmity borne to me — so also the domain of sex, and particularly the act of marriage, contains many elements that possess their analogues in the higher spiritual domain; for example, the elements of undivided application and complete surrender to the other partner, the element which may be characterized as an expansion or solution of strain, the element of ecstasy, and the element of self-disclosure and self-revelation. But this objective analogy of qualities is in itself no proof whatsoever of a real causal connection between an unreserved surrender which is purely spiritual and that comprised in the act of marriage. Still less does this analogy prove that all surrender, all expansion,

The distinction between male and female, the roots of which lie far deeper than the biological sphere, is certainly the presupposition alike of the power to complete and of the distinctive splendor of wedded love. But, on the other hand, the view that physical sex is a purely external addition to wedded love, in the sense that pride may be added to love, as, for example, to parents' love for a child, is equally false. On the contrary, I can understand the true significance and nature of physical sex only from above, from wedded *love*. The moment I treat physical sex as something complete in itself and take no account of its profoundest function, namely, in wedded love, I falsify its ultimate significance and become blind to the mystery it contains. Physical sex is certainly something distinct from love, but, nevertheless, between it and wedded love there subsists a pre-established harmony. Its true significance as an experience is inseparable from its character as the expression and flower of a specific kind of love.[2] The man who has grasped the meaning of sex recognizes its central position—intimacy and mystery—and understands the distinc-

---

all ecstasy, wherever found, are a sublimation of sex, a theory which not only substitutes a real connection for a qualitative analogy, but treats what is only the derivative and the copy as the original, indeed as the sole, reality. According to this view of the matter, the higher forms must be mere derivatives of the lower, nothing more than forms of sex veiled and decked out with fine feathers. This clearly is the logical result of that double mistake, as to the composition and structure of the human being, which thus avenges itself. On the other hand, it is certainly due to this qualitative analogy that sex can be the organic expression of a particular form of love and the field in which it finds fulfillment, though we must remember that here the analogy of qualities far exceeds these common formal elements. Nevertheless, when this function of the act of marriage is fulfilled, it constitutes immediately an entirely novel, real relationship between this love and physical sex, which, though bound up with the qualitative analogy, transcends it, but in which love is the point of departure, the actuating principle. On the other hand, in certain forms of sham love, where the parties are "in love" in the bad sense—cases of the kind which abound in erotic literature—there is actually a sublimation of the sex instinct. Unconsciously the true situation is dressed up, and behind the decoration the determining factor is sexual lust pure and simple. But this is no more true of genuine love than it is of art. Not all art, least of all genuine art, is a sublimation of the sex instinct because a certain type of erotic literature undoubtedly is. We are far from denying that suppressed sex can find its realization in a thousand and one other domains and assume a host of disguises. But these effects of repressed sex always bear the stamp of unhealthiness and aberration. We shall never find among them the forces and qualities which are vehicles of the highest values or are true to the norms of the spiritual life.

2. "The Church sees in married love the mutual attraction of the two sexes implanted by the Creator in human nature, and the foundation of and indispensable condition for the most intimate and the indissoluble community of life between human beings of different sex, and as such gives it her blessing." Franz Walter, *Der Leib und sein Recht in Christentum* (The Body and Its Rights in Christianity) (Donauwörth, 1910), Part 1, chap. 2, iii, p. 154. Ibid., p. 155: "What is the sex relation worth without pure strong love?"

tive quality of the act of marriage as uniting and amalgamating the partners, also the unique connection which subsists between physical sex and
wedded love and, moreover, knows why sex alone and not any other bodily function must enter into this combination.

The threefold purpose of marriage, *proles, fides, sacramentum* (offspring, fidelity, the sacrament), of which St. Thomas says: "*Primus finis
respondet matrimonio hominis, in quantum est animal; secundus, in quantum
est homo; tertius, in quantum est fidelis*" (the first end of marriage belongs
to man as an animal, the second as a human being, the third as a Christian), extends also to the act of marriage. That act has not only a function,
the generation of children; it also possesses a significance for man as a
human being *(in quantum homo)*—namely, to be the expression and fulfillment of wedded love and community of life—and, moreover, it par-
ticipates after a certain fashion in the sacramental meaning of
matrimony.[3] That is to say, the significance of physical sex in relation to
man *in quantum homo* cannot be purely utilitarian, functional in the narrowest sense, like its significance in relation to man *in quantum animal,* in
which its function is to produce offspring. On the contrary, in this connection we should rather speak of the meaning of sex than of its function. Speaking generally, we can talk only of a purely functional relation
when the content of anything is exhausted by its wholly objective finality, its actual production of a particular result. The function of the lungs
is to fill the blood with oxygen, the function of the eggshell to protect the
developing embryo. But in other cases the function, the finality, is not
simply an objective fact; it is at the same time the conscious motive of a
subject. For example, we undertake a journey with the deliberate intention of visiting a friend. The visit is not only the end of the journey, the
function it actually performs; it is also the purpose that we consciously
intend. The relation between physical sex and the interior purity of heart

3. The fact that the act of marriage also possesses a significance for man *in quantum homo*—
namely, the expression and fulfillment of wedded love—is of course no justification whatsoever for
an artificial divorce of this purpose from the function of generation. On the contrary, both constituents have been so organically united by God that to disrupt this unity by breaking this
mysterious and solemn bond between the different factors must be, on that account, if for no other
reason, a frightful sacrilege.

of a married pair is obviously not a functional relation in the strict sense, whether of the external objective kind or constituted by a purpose. The relationship, founded in the distinctive quality of both spheres, which enables the act of wedded communion to constitute and effect a union unique even in its psychological aspect, cannot be resolved into the far more formal and more mechanical relation of pure function; that is to say, of end and means. To regard wedded love as exclusively an objective means to the union of wedlock, and the latter in turn as a means to procreation, would be to subordinate entirely man *in quantum homo* to man *in quantum animal*—a thoroughly materialistic view.[4] On the other hand, to regard the marriage union as a means and wedded love as the end is equally impossible, because the marriage union already presupposes wedded love.[5] On the contrary, we are in presence of an entirely novel and most profound relationship which, as has been already hinted, must be conceived as a relation of significance. The act of wedded communion has indeed the *object* of propagation, but in addition the *significance* of a unique union of love. That this act, apart from the object just mentioned, is also significant for man *in quantum homo*, as the specific expression and fulfillment of wedded love and its longing for fuller communion, becomes particularly evident when we consider the significance which belongs to the *experience* of physical sex and to its distinctive quality, as perfecting or completing their subject. Compare, for example, eating. The significance of eating is exhausted by its objective end—the maintenance of life.

4. The bond between wedded love and physical sex can, of course, be *also* regarded as a means to procreation. But from this point of view it is impossible to discover the significance of sex for man *in quantum homo*, or give an account of what constitutes the special intrinsic meaning of the bond. This, on the contrary, must be sought in the significance of sex as expression and fulfillment. The fact that, in a world divinely planned, factors in themselves distinct and displaying on occasion an independent significance are also related as means and end, is no argument against the actual independence of their meanings. Indeed, the beauty of the functional harmony which prevails throughout the cosmos presupposes the independent significance of its diverse provinces, each with its distinctive *raison d'etre*. Otherwise the cosmos would be a barren machine.

5. As a consequence of the loose employment of the term "object" or "end" (*Zweck*) a relation such as exists between an experience and its expression or fulfillment is conceived as a relation of means and end, for no better reason than that the expression or fulfillment holds a subordinate position in respect of the experience which it fulfills. In reality, however, such a relationship is something totally different from the true relation of means and end, as becomes at once obvious when we consider the material character of the latter.

Whether or not we are conscious of the act of eating as an experience possesses no decisive significance. If throughout my meal my attention is wholly distracted elsewhere, absorbed by thoughts of some intellectual question or other, there is nothing whatever morally reprehensible, or even merely inappropriate, in my behavior. So far as the significance of eating is concerned it is of no practical consequence whether my attention plays any part in the process or not. For the act of wedded union, on the contrary, the question whether or not my attention is focused on what I am doing is by no means unimportant. From this act the factor of experience may not be excluded. If it is, the act becomes something morally reprehensible, indeed bestial. A fully deliberate conscious attention is demanded.

This in turn clearly proves that the act, over and above its universal function, possesses a special significance for man *in quantum homo*, which is not the case with eating, digestion, or breathing. Their significance is confined to man *in quantum animal*, and any conscious experience connected with them is merely an epiphenomenon or by-product. The pleasure which I receive from the taste of food can be safely regarded as being, so far as its intrinsic significance is concerned, simply a teleological means to the accomplishment of the objective end of nourishment. In this sphere also I can, it is true, sin by adopting a particular attitude toward this pleasure; for example, that of the glutton. And, no doubt, a general conscious intention directed to the object of eating is desirable, if for no other reason, because the ennoblement of all things by their reference to God, which is universally demanded, involves in this case a thankful consciousness of that object. But a complete unconsciousness of eating during the concrete act in any individual instance involves no essential violation of its significance, just because it possesses no special significance for man *in quantum homo*.

It is therefore evident that, apart from the relation of physical sex to procreation (*procreatio*), there exists a relation arising out of their respective qualities between physical sex and wedded love, which constitutes the significance of the former for man *in quantum homo*; a relation which, as contrasted with the utilitarian relation of means and end introduced from outside and constituting a purely external link, is, we have shown, a relation of significance which effects an intrinsic union. In virtue of its *quality*, physical sex is the expression of wedded love, and the specifically significant sphere of its fulfillment. And the act of wedded union is a unique expression of wedded love and its specific fulfillment, because in it both partners, according to the word of our Lord and Savior Jesus Christ, become *one* flesh; that is, they constitute a supreme unity, which wedded love seeks in a special fashion to attain. To overlook the union between physical sex and love or its significance and to recognize only the purely utilitarian bond between sex and the propagation of the race is to degrade man and to be blind to the meaning and value of this mysterious domain. Nor, so far as the essential is concerned, does this point of view become more rational if the utilitarian relation is also treated as the subjective purpose. The mere will to procreation is incapable of introducing into the act of wedded union the requisite element of conscious experience, for it neglects entirely the significance of the act for man *in quantum homo*—namely, *fides*. By itself this intention can never effect the organic bond between physical sex and the human spirit which lifts the act of wedded union out of the purely animal and biological sphere. Even if the intention to reproduce were invested with the noble purpose of giving the Church new souls, that intention by itself, to the exclusion of specific wedded love, could not organically unite physical sex with the heart and spirit, nor would it possess the power to inform from within the distinctive nature of sex, alloyed as it is by a tendency to overcome the spirit, and thus transform it into a positive good. The marriage act can only be transformed qualitatively and ennobled from within when the immensely powerful thought of the inception of a new human soul influences the physical act of sex through the medium of wedded love.

We will return later to the question: Which factor possesses the decisive power so to unite physical sex with the spiritual personality that the exercise of sex involves no falling away from God? Exclusive insistence upon the function of sex for man *in quantum animal* and the reduction of the connection between sex and spirit to a purely utilitarian relationship is, most of all, to be reprobated when it is a consequence of the method that explains everything by biological categories. Indeed, we must reject all overemphasis of biological points of view and the phenomenon of life; such, for instance, as we find in the so-called vital philosophy and, more generally, as a form of Modernism, that sacrifice of eternal truth to the spirit of the age.

And, finally, we must point out once again that sex is a mystery, though not, of course, in the theological sense of the term. It is in the first place a mystery in its quality as a sphere of mysterious experience. Of that we shall speak more in detail later. But apart from or in addition to this it is also a mystery inasmuch as the act of marriage signifies the mysterious creation of a new human being. It is no chance that God has invested that act with this creative significance. As God's love is the creative principle in the universe, so love is everywhere creation, and there is a profound significance in the nexus—at once symbol and reality— whereby from the creative act—in which two become one flesh from love and in love—the new human being proceeds. It was this thought that inspired the following prayer, taken from an old nuptial liturgy: "O Lord our God, Who didst create man pure and spotless and thereafter ordain that in the propagation of the human race one generation should be produced from another by the mystery of *love*."[6]

Here also we can do justice to the significance of this mysterious process only if we take the union of love into full account. It is possible to gauge in its fullness and depth the sublimity of the connection between sex and the origin of a new human being, or to recognize all that is implied by the fact that it is no mere living thing, but a man, who comes into existence,[7] if only we already understand the peculiar relationship that subsists between physical sex and wedded love.

Sex, however, is a mystery, even apart from the fact that it is the source

6. Cf. Fr. Athanasius Wintersig, *Liturgie und Frauenseele* (The Liturgy and the Soul of Woman), p. 89.

7. This is not affected by the fact that only in his body is man the product of union between the semen and ovum; the soul, on the contrary, is always God's immediate creation. For it remains true that the parents procreate a human body destined for the most intimate union with an immortal soul, and from which it actually receives its "form" (*anima forma corporis*; the soul is the form of the body).

from which a new human being proceeds. In its purely qualitative aspect also a mysterious character attaches, as we have already seen, to sex. That is sufficiently proved by its depth, centrality, and intimacy. In this domain man is faced at every turn by mystery. He surrenders himself after a unique fashion—encounters either the mystery of wedded love or the mystery of a terrible sin. Either the mysterious union of two human beings takes place in the sight of God (*in conspectu Dei*) or man flings himself away, surrenders his secret, delivers himself over to the flesh, desecrates and violates the secret of another, severs himself in a mysterious fashion from God. Mysterious, as the hallowed mystery whereby in marriage two become one flesh, is the abyss of sin to which the abuse of sex leads.

CHAPTER THREE

The Three Aspects of Sex

THE REMARKABLE FACT that one and the same function is the medium of the closest objective communion of two creatures and can be also the domain of fearful sin becomes more intelligible when we reflect that sex can present totally different qualities. Besides that quality, a blend of intimacy, centrality, mystery, and tenderness, which gives expression to a unique liberating surrender and unites in a fashion beyond words to describe, a peculiar fascination, alluring and intoxicating, can attach to sex. These two qualities are not inseparable, and, moreover, there is no intrinsic bond between them. On the contrary, up to a certain point they are mutually opposed. Sex possesses the tender, mysterious, ineffably uniting and intimate quality only when exercised as the expression of something more ultimate—namely, wedded love. As soon as sex is isolated and sought for its own sake its qualities are reversed. The depth, the seriousness, the mystery disappear, to make room for a fascinating, exciting, and befuddling charm which excludes anything beyond. Wherever sex is encountered in an unlawful form as a temptation there is heard this siren song of lust, with its honeyed poison. The sublime joy of ultimate surrender, touching, chaste, intimate, and mysterious, with which, under other circumstances, it is invested is completely absent. Sex is always extraordinary, but its characteristic extraordinariness assumes diametrically opposite forms. At one time it is awe-inspiring, mysterious, noble, chaste, and free; at another, illegitimate, intoxicating, and befogging. This becomes most evident if we consider the case when sex appears as not only specifically fascinating, but, as the domain of evil lust, addresses a diabolical appeal to man. No longer is there mystery, freedom, or tenderness; instead, we are in the presence of something sinister and oppressive; in an atmosphere where it is difficult to breathe. An entire world divides the extraordinariness of miracle from the twilight of magic, sinister and devilish. Both indeed are extraordinary, exceeding the scope of nature. But that which in the one case is bright, clear, awe-inspiring, illuminating, and holy, is in the other close, bemusing, eerie. So is it, *mutatis mutandis*, with sex. The quality of extraordinariness, which, of course, must now be understood in a purely natural sense, always attaches to sex so long as it is not directly misconceived. But what is in the one case mysterious is in the other uncanny; what in the one instance expands, in the other contracts. Sex possesses the former quality only so long as it functions as the pure expression of wedded love. The elements of intimacy, tenderness, and mystery, and the creation of a fundamental tie, which compose the true and divinely willed quality of sex, are accessible to him alone who beholds them in the closest union with wedded love and experiences them in a very special fashion as approved by God.[1] For the joy and attraction are here the result of the unique union, the mutual contact in the sexual sphere, the most intimate mutual self-donation and self-revelation, and, moreover, the consciousness of a union willed by God— all factors that are operative only when sex is exercised on the basis of wedded love. When sex is thus experienced there is no seduction in it, but liberation, pathos, and solemn earnest. On the other hand, the opposite quality of sex, its seductive magic, is not necessarily destroyed by its organic union with love. It can, indeed, even creep into the sanctuary of

---

1. For a detailed treatment of this decisive factor see chapter 6, sec. a.

marriage. But it is then a foreign element which contradicts the solemnity and tender sanctity of the wedded union. It distracts the attention from love. There is in it something irreverent and frivolous, degrading and corroding the soul. It is the tragedy of fallen man that the *danger* at least of this perversion is always present, the danger that sex should exercise over him this baser appeal. But to the degree in which the sublime aspect is present and is experienced by him the other vanishes. Even greater is the contrast between sex as the mystery of love and sex as the vehicle of diabolically evil lust. The mortal enchantment of evil lust is confined to sex when taken in isolation. It is the exact opposite of the quality that constitutes the joy and attraction of sex as the medium of the most profound union with another. The moment it sounds in a man's ear he is deaf to the voice of love, his heart becomes cold; for deep within himself he hears something essentially incompatible with love. Obviously, sex only reveals its true nature when it manifests the glorious qualities of intimacy, mystery, seriousness, and union; when, in other words, it comes to us as the fulfillment of wedded love invested with the consciousness of God's approval.[2]

2. A typical example of the distinction between the two negative aspects of sex—befogging charm and diabolic seduction—is to be found in Wagner's *Parsifal*. The flower girls represent the specific charm of sex when isolated; Kundry, on the other hand, its diabolic allurement.

CHAPTER FOUR

Impurity

HUMAN PURITY[1] involves a distinctive attitude to the important domain of sex. According to the attitude which a man adopts to sex he is pure or impure. If, then, we ask in what does impurity consist, the reply is easy: it consists in the abuse of sex.

In this connection several factors must be distinguished. In the first place *I fling myself away* by giving up this personal secret to another with no intention of a real and final surrender to that person or of entering thus into a lasting external union with my partner. Where the foundation has not been laid by wedded love and the deliberate purpose of forming a permanent objective community of life, secure from arbitrary whim, the act, which represents a unique self-donation and effects an intimate union of the most fundamental nature, signifies a specific squandering of self, the betrayal of oneself and one's partner. The evil (the neg-

---

1. We here confine ourselves of set purpose, not only to purity in the narrower sense, but, so understood, to purity as a human virtue. Purity in the wider sense, as also the purity of God and the angels, which indeed is the exemplar of all human purity, is reserved for treatment in later publications.

19

ative value) involved in the disharmony between the objective character of the act and the intention with which it is performed is obvious. This negative value, which such a flinging away of self involves, assumes its grossest form when the sensual pleasure has become a completely independent aim and the act is performed solely for its own sake, with no deeper relation to the other party. That man has become "one flesh with a harlot."

Besides this squandering of self, this betrayal of oneself and one's partner, which may be described as a specific *degradation* of both, this abuse of sex always involves a second factor, a *desecration*. To perform the act which signifies the hallowed union of two human beings in one flesh and should be the expression and fulfillment of a lasting and indissoluble bond of love—and which effects the most perfect self-surrender to another, because it involves the mutual revelation of a secret, a self-revelation, that is to say, of the most intimate character—with a partner to whom we are not united by the sacred tie of matrimony is obviously a desecration of the most awful kind. As all desecration is specifically sinful—for example, the abuse of a human being which I commit by treating him as a mere thing, thereby doing violence to his dignity as the image of God, the desecration of the Temple by the money-changers or of Holy Communion by receiving it from worldly motives—this particular desecration is also a sin. Moreover, this sinful desecration is not only committed by abuse of the act designed to express a lawful, profoundly solemn, and fundamental union of love, but is involved by every exercise of sex, whether with another or by oneself, apart from and in opposition to its lofty significance. As it is always a desecration to employ something destined for a sublime purpose in a fashion inconsistent with that noble object—as for instance to utter God's name thoughtlessly or irreverently —so is it in this case.

But not only is every abuse of sex a desecration; it further involves a specific defilement. And this brings us to the third factor from which impurity derives its evil, and indeed to that which most of all determines its distinctive quality.

Both aspects which sex displays immediately when it is isolated and no longer "formed" from within by wedded love and the consciousness of God's sanction—namely, the siren song of sensual attraction with its poisonous sweetness, and diabolic evil lust—display a peculiar power to corrode and defile the soul. The moment any man in his employment of sex "wills" one of these two aspects, and gives himself up to it, he incurs a mysterious defilement and separates himself in an altogether unique fashion from God. This quality, befogging, intoxicating, and infusing its poison into the very marrow of its victim, stands in peculiar contrast to the sphere of holiness, the home of liberation and sublimation, resplendent with the light of peace. And it further involves a specific opposition to the peculiar quality of expansive warmheartedness which belongs to pure love as such.

It is obviously beyond the power of language to describe sufficiently, or even "deduce," the evil inherent in the nature of sex when treated as its own end. All that can be done is to keep our gaze steadily fixed upon it. Its peculiar quality must be apprehended intuitively. For, apart from the universal impossibility of "explaining" and "proving" the distinctive nature of pure qualities, we are here faced with a secret of a quite special kind, since we are dealing with a fact the significance of which is rooted in a region beyond the normal field of our intellectual vision. We are face to face with the mystery of sex.[2] The fact, however, is too plainly visible to admit of doubt. Whenever sex is indulged for the sake of its sensuous appeal, and whenever it is withdrawn from its place in marriage and separated from its function as the expression of reverent and lawful wedded love, whereby, as we have seen, its quality is completely changed, the person concerned is defiled, his soul is made captive to the flesh, and a mysterious apostasy from God takes place, unmatched for its peculiar enigmatic quality by any other sin.

Finally, the abuse of sex also involves a special defilement of the guilty party when the nature of sex is misconceived and a man surrenders him-

---

2. We cannot therefore assign a "reason," in the strict sense of the term, why sex when treated as its own end emits this poisonous breath, though later on we shall consider the dangers peculiar to sex from the standpoint of man's formal structure. We are dealing here with factors which not only are bound up most closely with this distinctive quality of sex, but derive their drastic potency from it.

self to it unthinkingly simply as a source of pleasure. This is the case with the dull bestial impurity distinctive of the fleshly man.[3] Of those positive and negative aspects of sex which have just been discussed he perceives none. He misconceives the nature of sex, treating it exactly like the pleasure of the palate. He pursues the physical pleasure of sex solely for its pleasure, without understanding its peculiar nature. A man of this type falls below the level of the animal. Although in this case there is no surrender to the specifically "corrosive" quality of befogging charm or of diabolic evil lust—for *these* aspects of sex are not so much as conceived—there takes place, nevertheless, not to speak of the degradation and desecration, a defilement of an altogether special sort—a bondage to the flesh entirely different in kind from that involved, for example, by surrender to the pleasures of the table. Although the person concerned sees only a difference of degree between the pleasure of sex and other kinds of pleasure, the "sensualization" of the spirit which results from surrender to this pleasure differs not only in degree, but in quality, from the entirely different "sensualization" to which the glutton exposes himself. The havoc, incomparably further reaching and different in kind, here wrought upon the spirit, although the person concerned assimilates sex to the pleasure of eating, becomes intelligible when we consider the fundamental tendency to submerge the spiritual that belongs to sex when brought into full exercise.[4] This bestial surrender, unthinking and instinctive, to sexual pleasure as pleasure is a particularly gross instance of the submersion of the spirit in the physical. A person of this kind, however, is not submerged in the vital flood of his bodily life, like the sinner who yields himself to the specific charm of sex or to diabolic evil lust, but, in the dead physical substance of his body, is literally submerged in matter. And obviously this fleshly impure man is also distinguished from the glutton by the fearful desecration and degradation which his conduct involves.

No employment of sex, however, which is for any reason unlawful is free from impurity. Even if physical sex is not treated as an end in itself,

3. See further, chap. 3.
4. See further, chap. 1. See further the argument that for perfect purity a consciousness of God's express sanction is indispensable.

and the motive of the sexual act is, on the contrary, the desire for a genuine union of love, the sexual surrender not only involves a sin of disobedience, but, over and above that, a specific sin of impurity, whenever the union is forbidden on any ground whatsoever. For the moment a man defies a prohibition in the sexual sphere the union becomes in one way or another a passive yielding, a being carried away. This, it is true, does not mean that physical sex is directly made its own end, but it always involves an undue preponderance of the sensual factor. No other sphere is so sensitive to the touch of illegitimacy. Any breath of levity, any even momentary self-forgetfulness under the influence of passion, any abandonment to the passing moment, contradicts radically the significance of this union, its ultimacy, its seriousness and its irrevocability, and therefore always involves not only objectively, but *subjectively* also, a material impurity; indeed, in a certain sense, a desecration.[5]

A certain impurity in the narrower sense can indeed make its appearance even apart from the abuse of sex. This occurs when sexuality, entirely unknown to the party concerned, strays into other spheres and his attitude in these produces a certain sexual satisfaction which, however, is, of course, completely different from any actual physical realization of sex. We often come across men who will to be pure, who, wherever they recognize its presence, carefully avoid any conscious surrender to sex taken in isolation for its own sake, but who nevertheless are not genuinely pure, for they seek and find a certain sexual satisfaction in their love of excitement, their craving to make an impression, their sensibility, their self-importance, their carriage, the entire rhythm of their lives. Men of this type often consider themselves particularly pure, and speak of sex with disgust.[6] They consider themselves raised far above everything sexual, even perhaps despise the union of wedlock, because they consider it too

5. I am obviously not thinking here of any of those forms of perversion in which the gratification of evil lust is sought by surrender to certain things not in themselves sexual, e.g., cruelty in the case of a sadist. For a perversion of this kind does not represent any essentially new form of impurity over and above those already mentioned. Though some other domain is substituted for sex, it is made the vehicle of the diabolic charm to which the person concerned deliberately yields himself.

6. The Freudian hypothesis to which we have already referred has shed most valuable light on the problem presented by these types. Repressed sex is here the true explanation.

fleshly and themselves too precious to surrender their person to another in this fashion. Such men are often particularly prudish, and turn with disgust from anything in which the existence of sex finds open and unambiguous expression. Yet all the while their entire nature is charged with an oppressive sexuality; they live in an atmosphere of sexual constraint, and the manner in which they move, speak, and meet particular situations betrays the active presence of sex. It is obvious that this bondage to the spell of a negative sexuality cannot be treated as amounting to sinful impurity in the proper sense. Indeed, there is here, strictly speaking, no sin, but simply an imperfect general attitude, which roughly corresponds to the general attitude of pride which we find in the majority of men. This impurity involves no conscious surrender to sex, for there is no perception of its presence, no consent to its alluring charm, therefore no profanation of its specific secret. But, on the other hand, such men miss the peculiar freedom of the pure: the unconfined spirituality, the transparence, the radiance which is theirs alone. On the contrary, they are in bondage, their spirit is opaque and transmits no clear light, and they hang about every hole and corner in which sexuality lurks unbeknown. Their life is in fact passed in the conflict provoked by an unsatisfied attraction to sex in its negative aspects as bemusing charm or diabolic lust. Since they have never uprooted and overcome this attraction, nor even struggled against it in open combat, every other department of their life is infected and poisoned by this disposition. They are always unconsciously looking for a substitute, which they find more or less in many other forms by which life expresses itself.

CHAPTER FIVE

Purity and "Insensuality"

THE MERE absence of the impurity just described defines only the negative aspect of purity; it tells us nothing of its incomparable positive splendor. Thus, for example, we often meet with men wholly deaf to the appeal of sex, who, to be sure, do not defile themselves with any impurity, but who, nevertheless, cannot be termed pure in the full positive sense of the term. The alternative simply does not apply to them. We must therefore begin by making a sharp distinction between true purity and mere temperamental absence of sexuality, which may indeed involve the absence of positive impurity—though even this is not always the case— but which has nothing whatever to do with the virtue of purity. This cannot be overemphasized. For there are men for whom the lack of sexuality is an ideal and who place the perfection of purity in an entire absence of the "sex instinct." This is so remote from the truth that we cannot even regard insensibility to sex as an environment particularly favorable to purity.

To grasp this fully let us first of all consider the sense to be attached to the term *sinnlich*.[1] In ordinary usage the term is steeped in ambiguity. When someone is called *sinnlich*, the speaker may mean that he is susceptible to sex. But he very often means that all the physiological instincts of the man so described are powerfully developed. In contrast to those delicate ethereal natures whose instincts are mild and who therefore appear preeminently dematerialized and spiritual, although in the true sense this is not necessarily the case, or in contrast to those types which display a listless lack of vitality, we apply the term *sinnlich* to men richly endowed with fresh and vigorous life, whose vital instincts are powerful. This purely temperamental vigor of instinct can manifest itself in different fields, among them that of sexual passion. By itself it tells us nothing of its possessor's nature in other respects. For it is nothing more than a quality of temperament which can belong just as well to a spiritually minded person, who gives the first place to the things of the spirit, as to a debauchee. The spiritual man will endeavor to bring these instincts under the control of his will, and will not allow them to rule over him. The possession, therefore, of this temperament is no sign whatever that lust holds sway in the person concerned.

Nor does the fact that a man's instincts are powerful inform us in what way sex appeals to his temperament. There are, for example, men whose instincts are strongly developed, and in particular the sex instinct, who nevertheless lack all understanding of the peculiar quality of sex. They are completely blind to its mysterious and extraordinary character. For them its pleasure is as exclusively physical as, for example, the pleasure of eating. That is to say, sex appeals to them by none of the three qualities mentioned above, neither in its mystery and tender intimacy, nor in its seductive charm, nor as diabolic evil lust. Such men of powerful instincts, but with no understanding for the peculiarity of sex, cannot strictly speaking be called *sinnlich*; they ought rather to be termed *fleischlich* (fleshly). A "fleshly" temperament of this kind brings its possessor nothing of that sensitiveness and peculiar intensity of response which as

---

1. As this passage shows, there is no English word that covers the same ground. The translator could only omit this passage entirely or use the German word. He has usually rendered it "sexual." [Trans.]

purely temperamental factors accompany true sensuality.[2] On the contrary, it renders him particularly material, coarse, prosaic. Such a temperament is, properly speaking, alien rather than akin to the disposition we term *sinnlich*.[3]

We shall see this most plainly if we consider not those men whose fleshly temperament is held in subjection by a strong will, but those whose entire nature is dominated by this kind of appetite. Such men completely surrender themselves to their appetite both with their will and their entire emotional life. It rules them with undisputed sway. Such are those bestial men for whom life essentially consists in eating, drinking, sleep, and bodily pleasures of every description, and who are also immersed in sexual lust. Their entire being breathes a dull, fleshly atmosphere, proclaims a sluggish immersion in matter, a coarse insensibility. Everybody knows these unfortunate people, who are baser than the animals. They represent a type entirely different from those sinners who surrender to sex as the vehicle of a peculiar charm unlike anything else or of a diabolic evil lust, so that, strictly speaking, they should not be called temperamentally *sinnlich*.[4] They abuse sex, not by perverting its distinctive quality to evil, but because they utterly fail to perceive it; but, like the animals, they "make use" of sex. There is *Sinnlichkeit* in the strict sense only where there is a temperamental susceptibility to sex in its distinctive quality and as something extraordinary. This susceptibility always covers the entire field of sex and embraces everything connected with its secret; therefore, not only its immediate and purely physical sensations, but its psychophysical attraction. The man who is sensible to the peculiarity of sex in general, and in whom it is consciously or unconsciously operative as a simple disposition, derives from it at the same time a certain warmth and liveliness. As a pure disposition it is the counterpart in the vital sphere of temperamental alertness of intellect. In contrast to a

2. *Sinnlichkeit*.

3. In English such a temperament would certainly be called sensual. In this connection sensuous approaches closer to what is here meant by the German *sinnlich*. The fleshly man is certainly not sensuous. The man whose senses are highly developed, alert, and sensitive is. But our language does not make the precise distinction here drawn. [Trans.]

4. If sensual, they are not sensuous. [Trans.]

sluggish, phlegmatic temperament, it is accompanied by a lively susceptibility to impressions and ideas of every kind, by sensitiveness and alertness; above all, by intensity and delicacy of response. But this temperamental alertness only accompanies what is termed *Sinnlichkeit* when the word is used in its most definite sense, as the equivalent of "sexual." So far as this alertness is concerned, the question whether or not a man possesses a strong or weak instinctive life in general is irrelevant. But according to the character of the rest of the personality this sensual-sensuous or sexual (*sinnlich*) temperament assumes an entirely different aspect. Everything here depends on the question which of the three qualities of sex described above appeals to that particular person and what attitude he adopts in each instance to those qualities.

Corresponding to the different meanings of *sinnlich* are the many senses in which its opposite, *Unsinnlichkeit*,[5] may be understood. The term may denote the absence of strong instincts, as, for example, in the case of the ethereal type whose tender and at the same time sensitive nature gives us the impression that he is to a certain extent dematerialized. Here, however, we have to do simply with the temperamental opposite of *Sinnlichkeit* which cannot properly be called *unsinnlich*. In susceptibility to sex the preeminently sensual sphere is by no means necessarily involved. We might, however, use *Unsinnlichkeit* (insensuality) to denote a specific want of understanding for the peculiarity of sex such as we found it in the fleshly man, but which can exist equally well in men whose instincts are weak. And finally, the term might denote the absence of any susceptibility to sex, which in turn always involves a physical insensibility. This last case obviously excludes also a *temperamental* understanding of the peculiarity of sex. It does not, however, make it impossible to understand the positive and negative values attaching to the sexual sphere. An insensible person of this type is indeed deaf to the voice of sex, and the language in which its values are conveyed is not directly intelligible. But only this understanding of the language is immediately dependent on temperament. Such a person can quite well understand the

---

5. "Insensibility to sensual pleasure"; "insensuality," if I may coin this convenient negative. [Trans.]

sense of the words, and the value-qualities "pure" and "impure," though for the most part only indirectly and with the aid of the generic values of which these are species. For the understanding of these positive and negative values as such is dependent upon the general moral attitude. *Unsinnlichkeit* in this final sense, "insensibility to sex," which is what most people would understand by the term, is by no means to be identified with purity; on the contrary, as we have already hinted, it does not even present a particularly favorable environment for that virtue.

The strongest proof that purity and sexual insensibility (*Unsinnlichkeit*) are qualities which must be sharply distinguished is the specific spirituality which attaches to the pure, and is by no means a concomitant of insensibility, as such. (On the contrary, sexual insensibility in itself is the temperamental predisposition to an even greater "unspirituality" in a man's attitude toward sex. There are, for example, men of powerful and coarse instincts who are at the same time totally insensible to sex, and therefore *a fortiori* to its peculiar quality, men who live for eating, drinking, and sleep. They are too lazy and sluggish to be sexually responsive, too sleepy to possess the alertness which susceptibility to the peculiar quality of sex demands.)

But in any case the absence of a sexual temperament in no way connotes a particularly high degree of spirituality, any more than, *mutatis mutandis*, actual poverty connotes an interior independence of possessions. The pure man, on the contrary, is always characterized by a spirituality of a distinctive kind, which not only controls the vital and physical aspects of his being, but actually penetrates and spiritualizes them. In his case the spirit illuminates the entire man, his nature proclaims the triumph of the spirit over the flesh. The pure man is specifically spiritual, his nature displays not only the appearance of something ethereal and dematerialized, as is the case with the man whose passions are weak, but a *genuine* transcendence of matter, whereby he is made free of the realm of spirit. This, as we have seen, is not the case with the merely insensible, who may indeed be particularly material. Moreover, a distinctively prosaic atmosphere attaches to the latter. So long as he is merely insensitive to sex and not also pure, he is marked by a humdrum, prosaic drabness which is even legible in his face, and for the most part is entirely devoid of poetry or charm.

There are, of course, also humdrum people totally devoid of poetry, who nevertheless could not be called sexually insensible — *unsinnlich* in the radical sense. They are those fleshly men of whom we spoke just now. But prosiness and jog-trot dullness are certainly incompatible with sensibility to the distinctive quality of sex, *Sinnlichkeit* in the stricter sense.

In total contrast to the sexually insensible, the pure man is entirely free from this drabness. Instead of the dreary, humdrum atmosphere which surrounds the former, his being breathes an indescribable fragrance. He is invested with a unique radiance of spirit by which he is raised above the region of humdrum respectability and exerts a potent charm. Indeed, in the highest form of purity this radiance is such that in the poetry of his being he soars high above the sphere of its opposite, uninspired and uninspiring prose.

The sexually insensible is as such an incomplete man, to whom a very profound zone of human nature is closed. He lacks something indispensable to a complete humanity and, moreover, not something which is confined to the vital sphere, as, for example, moodiness, but something which colors the whole of his nature. For, as we have seen, sensibility to sex, as a temperamental disposition, goes far beyond the domain of sex and penetrates the entire man. The pure man, on the contrary, is the only man who is truly complete. In him a central orientation of human nature is fulfilled, and everything which the sexually insensible lacked he possesses in its entirety. But in this connection we cannot insist too emphatically that the man insensible to sex can obviously be at the same time pure, in which case both the dryness due to his insensibility and the "incompleteness," even to a residual defect of mere vitality, are removed by the luster of purity.

Here, however, we must not forget — for the distinction is of enormous, indeed, decisive, importance — that insensibility and sensibility to sex are purely and simply temperamental dispositions, like, for example, a lively or phlegmatic, a musical or unmusical, temperament. Purity, on the contrary, is never a temperament. This will become evident if we briefly consider what, precisely speaking, is meant by a temperament. In the strict sense a temperament, or subordinately a particular temperamental quality, is a personal idiosyncrasy which in no way depends upon a freely chosen general outlook or particular attitude, and involves nothing in the nature of an apprehension, affirmation, or rejection of values, but, like physical characteristics, is simply "given," and which, if capable of any alteration, can be altered essentially only by means in whose mode of operation the will plays no part. No doubt the part played by temperament can also be influenced by the person's freely chosen attitude— a temperamental sensibility can remain undeveloped or become starved —but the existence of that temperament is not thereby destroyed. Nor is the distinction between temperament and virtue in the very least affected by the fact that a temperament is not acquired. There is no lack of cases in which a man possesses a particular virtue from the very beginning of his moral life and has never acquired it. There are those who have been gentle from the nursery, others who have only become gentle by dint of long struggles. But in both cases alike, the gentleness is not temperamental in the true sense—in contrast to sham gentleness, lack of spirit, which is a genuine temperament, but also in contrast to the mild temperament due to weak passions, which, though it presents a favorable environment for the virtue of gentleness, has no claim to be regarded itself as gentleness. True gentleness is never a temperament, because it is always bound up with the fundamental orientation of the spirit, and because it is always accompanied by a loving attitude and by what that implies—a perception of the value of others as persons and a corresponding response: indeed, it also involves the will to be gentle and a characteristically delicate perception of the unloveliness, hardness, restlessness and malice inherent in anger and violence.

True gentleness, therefore, implies, and this is the most important point, a distinctive *apprehension of values* and a surrender to them which is more or less conscious according to the measure in which the gentleness is due to the soul's deliberate choices or to a natural disposition. But whether this surrender is difficult or easy, in either case there is here a genuine virtue, a section of morality, something grounded in the general moral attitude, not something which is simply "given."

We must guard against introducing into the concept of virtue the notion of achievement, and therefore admitting a virtue only where a particular moral attitude has been acquired by previous struggle. Otherwise we should be involved in the most ridiculous consequences, and the virtue of a St. John as compared with that of a St. Paul would not count as genuine virtue; indeed, the exemplar of all virtues, our Blessed Lady, could not be regarded as in the true sense virtuous, for she came from God's hand all beautiful (*tota pulchra*).[6] Therefore, in distinguishing between a natural disposition or temperament and virtue, we must, once for all, put aside as irrelevant the question whether the characteristic in question was only acquired in course of time and after a struggle, or by the grace of God belonged to the person from the outset, or was bestowed at a particular moment of his life. The distinction must rather be decided by the relation between the quality in question and the subject's fundamental moral position, by the degree to which it involves a perception of values and response to them, and is grounded in and upheld by the general attitude its possessor has freely adopted. Naturally, the distinction is also closely connected with the quality of the characteristic. Virtues are always of an entirely different quality from temperamental dispositions. A characteristic identical in quality cannot be sometimes a virtue, sometimes a temperament. No doubt there are temperaments which favor the development of particular virtues. For example, natures in which the instinctive life is weak are adapted by their temperament for spirituality, gentleness, patience, modesty, and so on. For natures whose instincts are stronger and more primitive these virtues are more difficult to attain. Courage, fidelity to truth once perceived, unreserved devotion of the entire person to what has been recognized as good, are, on the contrary,

---

6. In contrast to acquired virtue stand not only the virtue which attaches to a man from the outset, but that also which is bestowed upon him at one stroke in some moment of crisis. An instance of the latter is the conversion of St. Paul, when new ethical attitudes came instantaneously to birth in his soul which it would be quite impossible to regard as acquired, and which, nevertheless, were undoubtedly genuine virtues and not mere temperamental dispositions.

Even the virtue which slowly matures in us without conscious action on our part, but which at the same time is our reward for moral purpose and striving in other fields, cannot be termed "acquired."

the virtues which have affinity with this temperament. But these temperamental affinities do no more than render the corresponding virtue easier to attain and invite to its attainment, and though they may present a certain counterpart of the virtue on a far lower plane, they are not even its germ, for powerfully developed instincts are equally to be met with in the bestial debauchee who is the slave of his passions and possesses none of the above-mentioned virtues. Such temperamental dispositions in no way predetermine the virtue or otherwise of their possessor, whether a man's fundamental attitude is good or bad; they simply represent special paths already made which are equally at the disposal of a good or a bad moral attitude. They merely decide which vices and virtues are affine to the person concerned. But this affinity is not a decisive factor. For there are men, for example, who in spite of strong passions are markedly spiritual, gentle, and patient, as was very often the case with the saints.

All this is but further proof that a quality of temperament can in no case be regarded as a virtue, any more than a genuine virtue, though it has not been acquired, can be explained as a mere temperament. Truthfulness, justice, purity, patience, gentleness, kindliness, humility, may be "natural" virtues in contrast to fully conscious virtues, which are in the strict sense products of the spirit—a distinction obviously accompanied by a profound difference of quality, which we must discuss in greater detail later.[7] But mere temperaments they can never be. Their distinctive positively ethical and rationally illuminated quality, their specific beauty, necessarily depends upon their formal character as virtues, a character which is enhanced in so far as a virtue is the deliberate product of the spirit. As we have already hinted, the distinction between virtue and temperament is very largely determined by the part played by the person in their respective production or maintenance. Every virtue, even if from earliest youth it has simply existed without a struggle, is "supported" by the spiritual person in virtue of his fundamental attitude or ethical position. It can therefore exist only so long as that person in some way or

7. We shall then see the significance possessed by this difference of quality within the sphere of the virtues. Meanwhile, we cannot too strongly emphasize the fact that even the less conscious natural virtue is wholly different from its temperamental counterpart of which we have just spoken.

other freely cooperates in its production. This is due to the fact that every virtue involves a habitual response to some value. For example, the humble man apprehends God's infinite majesty and incomparable sublimity; he yields himself wholly to God and will be nothing of himself but only from God and to His glory. The truthful man perceives the inner beauty of truth and the loathsomeness of deceit, lies, and trickery. The instant the person renounces this habitual response to a value and replaces it by indifference or even hostility to that value, becomes wholly dominated by pride or lust in his fundamental habitual attitude — his virtue is immediately lost. There is therefore no virtue which a man cannot lose. If, for example, a man yields himself wholly to evil, falls away from God, making himself his end instead of God, breaks away completely from the sphere of values, so that his attitude is no longer one of response to ethical value, but proud and lustful, all his virtues cease *ipso facto* to exist as such.

With a mere temperament the case is altogether different. There are, no doubt, many cases in which a man loses some particular quality of temperament, but never as the result of a change in his fundamental moral attitude. Such changes are, on the contrary, produced by causes that lie wholly outside the sphere of volition, which gradually or suddenly destroy the temperament in question. And the more a temperament is physiologically conditioned, the more physiological are these non-volitional causes. The lively energetic temperament produced by a strong vitality can be destroyed by over-fatigue, narcotics, dissipation, illnesses, and so on, as also by excessive misfortunes. But it can never be destroyed from within by changes in the fundamental moral attitude. Or, again, a musical temperament can be destroyed by drink, illness, and so on, but as a pure temperament it is never dependent upon the person's freely chosen attitude to the world of values.

With respect to the acquisition of virtues and temperaments the position is similar. Every virtue can be acquired with the help of grace, its germ being always a free response to value. If, for instance, an angry, violent man becomes gentle, the change must involve the victory of the appropriate response to value, whether that victory be won by a protracted struggle or whether by a special grace of God the person in question overcomes his violent temper at one blow. Indeed, the distinction between temperaments and virtues is shown most clearly by the fact that the former can never be in this sense acquired. It is, for example, impossible to acquire by any means whatsoever such specific talents as a musical or mathematical aptitude.

These general distinctions between temperaments and virtues which have now been explained throw further light on the distinction between purity and sexual insensibility (*Unsinnlichkeit*). As we have already pointed out, that insensibility and purity are totally distinct is evident at the first glance, from the fact that insensibility is a pure quality of temperament, purity a typical virtue; and it is equally impossible to identify sensuality (*Sinnlichkeit*), in the sense of strong susceptibility to sex, with impurity. Such sexual insensibility consists simply in the lack of susceptibility to the entire domain of sex, it involves no particular attitude to the sphere of purity and impurity. The insensible man is incapable of understanding the positive and negative significance attaching to sex, just as the man without a musical ear is incapable of grasping the qualities which belong to the world of musical notes. For the man who is completely unmusical the most trivial commonplace melody and the noblest are equally a meaningless noise. Similarly, in sexual insensibility, as such, there is no perception whatsoever of the positive or negative values which belong to the domain of sex and therefore, of course, no attitude of response to them; neither an acceptance of the positive values of sex nor a rejection of its negative values. In complete contrast to this the virtue of purity essentially involves a specific perception of the positive and negative values attaching to sex, and a corresponding positive or negative response. This by itself is sufficient to reveal the profound difference between purity and sexual insensibility.

But not only are insensibility and purity in no way identical; insensibility, as we have already pointed out, does not even constitute an environment particularly favorable to the virtue of purity. For it is not even the temperament which is affine to that virtue and which makes it easier. That is to say, it is not the temperamental counterpart of purity. It is

related to purity as a phlegmatic temperament to gentleness, not as weak
passions to gentleness. We shall see this most clearly when we ask what
is the temperament which makes the virtue of purity easier and is, in a
sense, its counterpart. This, we shall find, is *also* the opposite of the *fleshly*
temperament; namely, a general softness of the passions, a universal delicacy of feeling, sensitiveness—that temperament which, as we saw,
strikes us as spiritual, free from the grossness of matter. Not the absence
of sensibility to sex, but weak, as opposed to strong, passions that determine the temperament must be regarded as the environment most favorable to purity.[8] On the contrary, if sensibility to the appeal of sex
accompanies a temperamental delicacy of feeling, not only does it not
change the nature of the latter as an environment favorable to purity, it
actually enhances it. For a temperamental susceptibility to the distinctive
quality and extraordinary character of sex of its very nature renders it easier to understand the positive and negative values which can be realized
in this sphere, an understanding which the sexually insensitive must
acquire from outside and indirectly, if he will attain the virtue of purity.[9]
And, finally, there is required as a constituent of the temperamental counterpart of purity something which also constitutes the temperamental
support of modesty—namely, the delicate refined temper which in no situation yields the reins to any clamorous and unrestrained passion; the
instinctive reserve which shrinks from exposing its secrets to the glare;
and an impulse to shun the uncanny aspect of sex and draw back from it.

8. The only service rendered by a radical insensibility to sex is the absence of actual impurity in
the narrowest sense of the term. No doubt the man wholly insensitive to sex will not feel the tainted
breath of sex, taken as its own end—will not surrender to a charm of which he knows nothing. But
he may quite well be impure in a wider sense. He may, for example, wholly fail to understand the
moral evil of impurity, and approve of impurity in others, as being, for example, the free, unfettered
expression of one's natural instincts. Sex, indeed, even in its purely exterior aspect, has the appearance of something extraordinary, so that even to one who in consequence of a fleshly or a radically
insensible temperament is deaf to its language it displays significant warning signals. The sexually
insensible can therefore be impure, even in the narrower sense, if, as the result of a shameless attitude,
they pay no heed to these signals for whose apprehension a general delicacy of feeling is sufficient.
    From no point of view is sexual insensibility favorable to the positive virtue of purity, as I shall
now proceed to show.
    9. This is obviously true only of human purity. The purity of the angels is a purity in which the
conditional indispensability of sexual sensitiveness for the understanding of the possible values of
sex, positive and negative, is transcended per eminentiam.

It has now been established beyond the least doubt that sexual insensibility and purity differ *toto caelo*, and no one is pure simply because he is insensible. The man who is insensible to sex can in certain cases be *impure*, although impure only in the wide sense of the term,[10] and this wider impurity is wholly incompatible with the genuine virtue of purity in that strict sense in which, for our purpose, it is essential to understand it. As insensible to sex he stands outside the sphere of the alternative *pure* or *impure* in the stricter sense of the terms. His purity or impurity depends upon factors as to whose presence insensibility decides nothing, either positively or negatively. Since, as we have seen, insensibility, apart from its significance for purity, is in itself a defect, for it involves the absence of a certain warmth, liveliness, and so on — it is as such a disvalue, though, since it is a mere temperament, not a moral disvalue. It would therefore be absurd offhand to declare sexual insensibility a desirable condition, let alone to regard it as the culmination, of purity.

10. We can also, as we mentioned at the outset, understand purity in a quite general sense. Discussion of the relationship between the general virtue of purity in its diverse forms to purity in the stricter and strictest sense must be reserved for later publications.

CHAPTER SIX

Purity as a Positive Virtue

(a) The attitude of the pure

The pure man perceives the mystery of sex. He perceives its depth, its seriousness, its intimacy—whether because, temperamentally awake to these qualities, he apprehends intuitively the character of sex, or because, temperamentally unaware of them, he knows it rather from the outside. He understands implicitly the sublime purpose and fundamental significance of sex, and perceives the fearful profanation which every abuse of sex represents, the deadly poison, defiling the soul and separating it from God, which sexual pleasure generates when treated as its own end. He is marked by a profound shrinking from any contact with sex as soon as it is thus isolated and rendered poisonous. He possesses a deep reverence for the mystery of which he is here in the presence. Sex as such in no aspect seems to him contemptible or base. Bearing no repugnance to the fact of sex, free from all prudish and hysterical disgust, whether of sex as such or of the act of marriage, he remains at a respectful distance from it so long as he is not called by the disposition of God to enter its domain. *Reverence* is a fundamental component of purity. The pure man always lives in an attitude of reverence for God and His creation, and therefore reveres sex, its profundity, and its sublime and divinely ordained meaning. Indeed, and we have now reached the factor which is decisive both for purity and for the character of sex, the pure man understands that sex *belongs in a special manner to God*, and that he may only make such use of it as is explicitly sanctioned by Him. Only with God's express permission may he eat of the fruit of this tree. Nothing reveals more plainly the presence of a mystery than this need of a special sanction from God to enter the sexual domain. In contrast to the innocuous sphere of eating and drinking, or that of intellectual activity, the domain of sex belongs in a unique fashion to God. To be sure, in his employment of all earthly goods man must regard himself as God's steward, not as his own master. Here, however, an entirely new factor comes into play. This sphere, in virtue of its depth and mystery, is reserved in an altogether special fashion to God, and man, even within the permitted bounds, is not simply free, as in other spheres, to do whatever seems good to him. Moreover, this mystery which attaches to sex, even as an objective reality, results from its quality as revealed in experience, even if we leave out of account the fact that it is the mysterious seat of propagation, though the latter sets the mystery of sex in a particularly vivid light, and stands in a profound intrinsic connection with it. Man must feel for sex an awe which no other sphere demands — an awe which permits his access only if God in a special fashion should give him leave, as He gives it in the *sacrament* of matrimony. For the truly pure man the bond with wedded love and the intention of a common life to last till death are not sufficient; he requires further the specific consciousness of God's express sanction, the knowledge that it is only by divine permission that he lifts the veil from this mystery, an attitude which can be paralleled elsewhere in the religious sphere. And even when he may lift the veil, he will never abandon himself without restraint to the pleasure of sex. To be sure he may — indeed, he should — surrender himself without reserve to the beloved, but not to the specific quality of sex. The latter always demands, even when it is entirely positive, a reverent awe; and demands it to be "formed" by being brought into explicit relation to

God.[1] The pure man guards his secret, never lifts the veil unbidden. He is always modest. But his modesty has nothing that savors of self-importance, whether of conduct or feeling. He does not guard the secret by simply concealing it from others while he revels in it himself and in so doing feels himself somehow important. That is the attitude of the prude. With the pure you never breathe this oppressive atmosphere. Simple and open, he is distinguished by a limpid radiance of soul. He remains at a distance from his secret so long as God does not call upon him to unveil it. With spirit serene and bright and in an attitude of humility he leaves it in God's hand. We are here brought face to face with an absolutely essential element of purity. In a special sense the pure man walks with God. He never departs from the Divine Presence. He does not hide himself from God, like Adam after the Fall. *He will never consent to anything incompatible in its quality with the light of holiness which shines upon us from the countenance of Jesus.* Within his soul an indefinable "something" always abides in unclouded light; his spirit is neither corroded by the intoxicating poison of sex as its own end, nor infected by the oppressive sultriness which distinguishes the zone of evil lust. His soul is steeped in a peculiar light, radiant and clear; there is in him no twilight or dusk; he is surrounded by no atmosphere heavy with poisonous perfume and in which it is impossible to breathe freely. No cloud darkens his spirit as it "shines" before God. As we have already seen, the pure is distinguished by the rich plenty of his spiritual endowment. The specific beauty attaching to the unclouded luster of a soul which has come from God's hand, has been redeemed by Christ, and is the likeness of God—the beauty, that is, of the spiritual person—shines out upon us from the pure. The pure man remains a vessel in which the light which flows forth from God can unfold without obscuration; his soul shines before God, because it reflects His glory. Moreover, a peculiar peace has possession of his entire being; not inwardly alone, but outwardly to the world his soul reflects something of His peace who is called "our peace and our reconciliation." But only the soul that is filled

1. Wherein precisely this "forming" consists will appear more clearly when we discuss the specific purity of marriage.

with *love* can be pure in this positive sense; the cold and proud spirit can never possess this unclouded light.[2]

Purity is further characterized by a humble sincerity. The pure man feels himself a sinner capable, but for the help of God's grace, of being submerged at any moment by the flesh. With the heathen poet he confesses, "*Homo sum, humani nihil a me alienum puto*" (I am human, and nothing human I consider foreign to me). He does not shrink from looking the dangers which surround him full in the face. He never forgets that "the devil goeth about as a roaring lion, seeking whom he may devour." He does not imagine himself made of other material than flesh and blood and inaccessible to the weakness of the flesh. Remote from him, too, is the false modesty of the prude, who refuses to admit the existence of these dangers for himself or others. And his attitude continues the same even if he has never experienced sexual temptations. For simplicity, sincerity, and humility are almost as essential to true purity as is reverence.

(b) The pure man's specific perception
of value and his response to it

As we have already seen, every virtue involves a perception of value and a response to it. Which, then, are the values in whose contemplation the pure man lives and to which purity implies assent?

In the first place every complete virtue which is the product of the spirit involves a perception and understanding of the positive value of the virtue itself and the negative value of the opposite vice. The pure man perceives and understands the value of purity. Whenever he meets a pure man his purity is perceived by him as a positive value, its fragrance delights him, and its beauty is understood. Whenever he meets an impure man he perceives the negative value of his impurity, and the disfigured

---

2. This raises an extremely important question. Which other virtues demand purity as the condition of their existence? What, for example, is the nature of the close connection that exists in the first place between purity in the stricter and purity in the wider sense, in the second place between purity in the wider sense and other virtues? As we have already pointed out, a fuller treatment of this question exceeds the scope of the present work.

and disease-pocked countenance of that man's soul pierces his heart with anguish. Obviously, there is no question of a reflex perception of his own purity. As with every other virtue, so here, a reflex glance at the possessor's own worth is sufficient to endanger the attitude which is the foundation of all virtue—namely, humility—and directly contradicts it if that glance involves in any way a consciousness that he possesses the virtue in question. But the humble man nevertheless recognizes the intrinsic beauty and incomparable value of humility, and not only in other men individually, as a particular value in them, but universally as the virtue humility. It is the same with the pure. Nevertheless, not only a recognition by the understanding of the virtue of purity is characteristic of the pure man, but also an attitude of assent to that value, both an actual response to it in each individual case of contact with purity, and a habitual response to purity. The pure man lives, so to speak, in the sight (*in conspectu*) of God's purity, the fountainhead of all purity, and responds to it with the permanent and habitual assent of his will. It sets his heart on fire; he *loves* it.

The pure man—we are speaking of the complete virtue which is a product of the spirit—always recognizes and loves purity, just as he understands impurity in its negative value and abhors it. But this understanding of purity itself and assent to it, which is inherent in the virtue of purity, is not the sole perception of value and response to it that purity involves. The perception of value and the response which we have just described is rather one which accompanies purity than that which itself constitutes the virtue. The just man, for example, will always understand the value of justice and *will* justice, but the value to which he responds when he behaves justly, the value the response to which formally constitutes justice, is not the value of justice itself. Otherwise we should be involved in an infinite regress. When anyone behaves justly he envisages the real obligations bound up with the sphere of objective rights; he has in view the value which consists in the fulfillment of these real obligations, and he wills it.

What, then, is the specific value, or valuable quality, which the pure man, as such, envisages and *wills*? It is the splendor which attaches to everything united indissolubly with God the Holy of Holies, and pre-eminently to that which reflects the light of holiness, which the pure man beholds, on which his gaze is fixed unswervingly. The brightness of His countenance to Whom the angels chant their Trisagion, which is, indeed, incompatible with any negative value, that is, with anything evil, but stands in special opposition to particular evils, is apprehended by the pure in its clear, resplendent, and immaculate beauty, and willed by an unreserved surrender. It is the surrender to this splendor which formally *constitutes* purity. We are now better able to understand why the pure lives more than others in God's presence. His countenance is turned to God, and he rejects everything which would compel him to fly from His face, everything whose nature is in any way incompatible with this splendor and cannot endure the divine gaze. We can point to no specific value, or valuable quality, the assent to which makes a man pure. It is rather a quality which belongs to all genuine values, and that moreover in proportion to their rank in the scale of values, and particularly to the immediacy with which they are related to God and the sphere of holiness. But to constitute the real virtue of purity, positive, complete, the product of the spirit, a perception of the luster *common* to all genuine values is insufficient; a perception of the splendor of holiness in particular, of the light peculiar to the supernatural alone, and a surrender to this value precisely as such, are also essential. We shall shortly discuss this point in greater detail.

The *negative value* whose rejection is among the factors which constitute purity is of a far more special nature. Here it is not simply a question of the darkness which attaches to every negative value, nor even of the defilement common to every moral evil, but of a specific category of negative values which are distinctively and diametrically opposed to this light, and which in a special manner defile the man who yields himself to them and banish him from God's countenance. The virtue of purity, as we have already seen, involves on the part of its possessor a distinctive attitude to sex. The abiding interior rejection of the negative values which attach to sex as soon as it becomes its own end and makes its appeal to us as the seat of a bemusing charm, diabolic evil lust, or a coarse pleasure of the flesh, is specifically characteristic of the pure. Moreover, this rejection must proceed from an understanding of the special nature of these qualities, as a canker eating into the soul and excluding the fragrant breath of the Spirit, and of the abyss which opens, and the banishment from God's face which necessarily ensues, when man surrenders himself to them. The pure man is aware of the negative value attaching to sex as its own end, whether or not he has an ear for its seductive language. He grasps the mystery of the poison here concealed—its potency in effecting a unique separation from God—and with his whole soul rejects, indeed, flies from it.

We might be tempted to suppose that as purity is born of rejecting the negative values of sex as its own end, it is specifically constituted by surrender to the positive values of sex when, according to the Divine Ordinance, it expresses the union of wedded love—by the correct response to sex in its double aspect as the subject of positive and negative values—and hence that the values attaching to sex are the specific objective correlate of purity. This would, however, be a mistake. The value which attaches to sex when it fulfills its divinely ordained function, as mysteriously tender, affecting, liberating, and creating a bond of a specific kind, is the objective correlate of other virtues, for example, depth, tenderness, and a particular kind of self-devoting love. Purity, no doubt, involves an understanding of these values and of the principles on which they are based, and demands that the employment of sex should be a surrender to these values alone. Indeed, such an employment of sex *is* specifically pure; but it presupposes purity as already in existence. It is, indeed, *a* realization of purity; but it is not *the* realization, and the response to these values does not *determine* the content of purity. Here, too, purity consists primarily in this, that the person who possesses it never cuts himself off from the splendor which shines upon him from the countenance of Jesus, but, on the contrary, wills in the domain of sex only that which has no need to hide from His light and in no respect opposes it. No doubt, a particular attitude to the distinctive positive values of sex is also always inherent in specifically human purity, and sex is in a peculiar fashion coordinated with purity; but how little purity consists in explicit surrender to these values in intention, still less in act, is evident from this fact alone, that virginity, when chosen in obedience to the Divine Will, is the ideal form of purity.

The significance for purity which, speaking generally, attaches to the positive values of sex is seen most clearly when purity is compared with chastity. Chastity, which we cannot discuss in greater detail here, on the one hand is clearly *different* from purity, and on the other hand is inseparably bound up with human purity. Chastity is exclusively concerned with sex. To guard the secret of sex is its life and soul. Chastity cannot be attributed to sexless beings, for example, the angels. But the angel is an exemplar of purity. We speak of the "girdle" of chastity, and the symbol expresses its character perfectly. Chastity means keeping the sexual secret hidden, as a domain the disposition of which lies in God's hand. It is a virtue whose positive quality is created by the avoidance of something negative. In man, chastity, as we can easily understand, is at once a presupposition and a result of purity, but it covers a far more restricted ground. It is concerned exclusively with sex, and consists *solely* in a right attitude to sex, whereas purity consists in a more general response to value. The symbol of the latter is not the protective girdle or the fortress which secludes and guards, but unsullied whiteness, the lily, unclouded light.

From the comparison between purity and chastity two results emerge. On the one hand it proves that purity does not, like chastity, consist primarily and necessarily in an attitude to sex, but primarily in an abiding in God's presence and a surrender to the glory of His countenance. But it shows us on the other hand that *human* purity does, first and foremost, imply and demand a particular attitude to sex. Hence, although sex is not the objective correlate of purity, and purity, therefore, does not consist in the response to it as, in a certain sense, is the case with chastity, nevertheless sex does possess a peculiar significance for purity. That this is the case is sufficiently shown by the fact that, in man, purity necessarily involves chastity. Chastity is, so to speak, the perfect development of one element of human purity. It exercises a ministerial function with respect to the latter so that we may say that *in order to be* pure a man must be chaste. It is purity which gives his attitude its significance, for the point of view which determines his assent to sex *is* — not the possible objective values it may present — but purity itself. He guards his secret in defense against everything which is opposed to purity.

Nevertheless, its specific response to the mystery with which the domain of sex is invested confers upon chastity a relative independence and a beauty peculiar to itself.

(c) The indispensable supernatural foundation of purity

To understand the nature of purity in the strict sense, the purity which is the product of the spirit, we must now show that it is among the virtues which require a supernatural foundation.

There are, indeed, men who have about them something undefiled, which reminds us of nature in her virgin state. They avoid sex, isolated as its own end with its tainted and oppressive atmosphere; they can breathe only in the clear, open air. But they lack that spiritualization of the entire man, "the spiritual riches," which characterizes perfect purity. Their purity seems rather the manifestation of a splendid untarnished vitality, though this natural purity is, of course, never something *merely* vital, but extends also to the moral sphere. Nevertheless, the atmosphere which invests it, and which we breathe in the presence of a naturally pure man in contrast to the potent spirituality of the purity which is begotten of the spirit, is the nobility of life unsullied and uncorrupted, as it were, fresh from the hand of God.

Nature's pure men have about them something of the purity of the mountain torrent, something of the clear, fresh air of early morning, but nothing which substantially transcends this world and moves in a higher region. Unlike those whose purity is born of the spirit, their being is not redolent of something "not of this world." Obviously a gulf divides this natural purity from the virtue just described, a product of the spirit in the strict sense, which alone has, strictly speaking, the right to the name of purity. Nevertheless, this natural purity is something wholly positive, beautiful, and attractive. It is far more than the mere temperamental counterpart of purity. We have already pointed out that these natural virtues must not be confused with qualities of temperament. Even this merely natural purity, then, is beautiful and lovable, and it has a moral value which does not belong to the merely temperamental counterpart of purity. It is not, like a quality of temperament, material for virtue to work upon, but an actual constituent of its possessor's distinctive character and being.

The distinction between natural purity and the temperament which we have indicated as its favorable environment consists essentially—and this holds good of all natural virtues and the corresponding temperaments—in the fact that the temperament involves no attitude of the person, still less any perception of value and response to it. The natural virtue of purity, on the contrary, as contrasted with its temperamental counterpart, involves an explicit perception of value. The naturally pure man is sensible in a particular instance of the impurity of a situation, person, book, and so on; moreover, it always presents itself to him as a negative value. And what is even more important than the perception of this negative value, he *rejects it* and turns away whenever he breathes this tainted air. He feels ill in an impure atmosphere. No one can help seeing that this consciousness and rejection of impurity is radically different from the temperamental shrinking from sex that we sometimes find in tender and highly sensitive men and women. Even the vital shrinking of the virgin from surrendering her virginity, even in marriage, is a temperamental disposition of this kind, which does not constitute purity. It manifests the proud reserve of an untamed nature, which rejects not the negative values incident to sex, but incidental features of neutral value, especially the subordination to another that the sexual surrender involves. Or it may be the violent, exciting quality of sex which is rejected. The naturally pure man, on the contrary, genuinely rejects the negative value of impurity.

If natural purity is thus distinguished—by its perception of the values, pure and impure, and its rejection of the impure in any given instance—from every merely temperamental disposition that renders purity easier, on the one hand, and, on the other hand by *the fashion* in which it perceives and responds to these values, it essentially contrasts with the perfect virtue of purity. Nature's pure men are sensible of the impurity of sex when made an end in itself and its purity when not thus abused; they approve the latter and reject the former. But their perception of values lacks two factors of decisive importance. In the first place it is simply a perception of the particular concrete value, positive or negative, then and there present; it is not a knowledge of the value of purity, a permanent knowledge of the virtue, for which the perception of values in each particular instance is simply a concrete exemplification or realization of a habitual contact with the values in question. Secondly, even the concrete perception of value by the naturally pure is not, strictly speaking, a matter of principle. Their understanding of the value of purity is too superficial to reveal to them its full seriousness, and its self-sufficient majesty; they fail to grasp that surrender and assent are *due* to it, as such, whatever may be their natural inclination. They are, in short, morally unconscious men, men who have not yet attained ethical maturity, whose attitude, therefore, lacks the sanction of the central personality, the free spiritual self.[3] They have not awoken to that freedom which confirms or rejects the judgments of their nature. Even when their attitude is a response to value, they are, as it were, merely voicing their nature. Their perception of value and response to it are still alloyed with an element of chance.

Moreover, their natural purity consists in assent to a value which differs essentially from that on which the gaze of the man whose purity is a product of the spirit is turned. Whereas in the case of the latter it is the splendor which shines from the countenance of God, the thrice Holy, in the case of the naturally pure it is the free, clear air of nature in contrast to the oppressive, sickly, and poisonous atmosphere of sex, isolated as its own end. People of this sort usually display an antipathy to anything artificial or over-refined, and possess a subconscious feeling of solidarity with nature, with her truth, her simplicity, her clarity.

Besides the natural purity described above there is also a ritual purity of the natural order which plays an important part in most religions.[4]

3. See further the section of the author's "Sittlichkeit und ethische Werterkenntnis" (English translation, *Morality and the Perception of Ethical Values*, forthcoming from Hildebrand Press), *Jahrbuch für philosophische und phänomenologische Forschung* (Halle, 1922), in which the question of fundamental attitudes is treated.

4. Cf. Joseph Muller, *Die Keuschheitsideen* (Notions of Chastity).

Among many races, sexual continence is regarded as indispensable for religious functions and offices, and a connection of one kind or another is held to exist between purity and ritual holiness. But in contrast to natural purity, this ritual purity has no claim whatever to be considered a virtue. For in this case the subject of the purity is neither the person as such, nor his attitude, behavior, or disposition. *Physical continence*, as such, the avoidance of actual contact with sex, is for one reason or another regarded as *materia consecranda* (material to be consecrated). As the sacrificial victim must be unblemished, the gifts offered to God, the vestments and the altar, pure, so must it be with the person consecrated to God. There is thus no essential difference between the purity of a thing to be consecrated to God and this heathen ritual purity of the person. It is further characteristic of this purity that no distinction is made between virginity and purity, although the value of virginity is no better understood than the value of purity.[5]

As the principal motives for regarding sexual "inviolacy" as essential for consecration to God we may mention the following. First, the preciousness of the unopened bud. This preciousness, as here conceived, is wholly vital and physiological; it is analogous to the preciousness of youth, something which, even from the standpoint of physical sex, possesses a peculiar charm. The creature which is to be consecrated to the Deity and given over to Him in a special fashion must not lack this excellence.

Secondly, emancipation from all other ties; being wholly at the disposal of God, completely unused. As the value of every gift is enhanced, if it exists solely for him to whom it is given, fulfills no other purpose, is and remains unused, so the person is here entirely regarded as a thing consecrated to God.[6] To make the sexual surrender is to anchor oneself most firmly to the world and to enter into the closest union with one's fellow creatures. Therefore, it is precisely in this respect that the man who is consecrated to God must be inviolate.

5. See further the second part of this work: Virginity.
6. This presents no analogy to St. Paul's undividedness, since here the being of the person qua person is completely left out of account—whereas St. Paul's *indivisus est* (1 Cor. 7:3 2–34) is wholly concerned with the disposition of the man who decides to give himself to God, that is to say, entirely regards the person as such.

And lastly there is an obscure sense of the danger of sex. Its power to destroy, disintegrate, and devour is dimly felt, that baneful potency with which it is charged when, as is necessarily the case here, it is viewed apart from the antidotes and sublimations that Christian ethics alone can supply. The man consecrated to God must avoid this danger. But here also this avoidance is simply a matter of external conduct, not of interior disposition. It is, therefore, impossible to regard it as even a natural, let alone a spirit-begotten virtue.

The natural virtue of purity is thus sharply distinguished from purity in the strictest sense, the virtue which is a product of spirit. But we have already pointed out that the perfect spirit-created virtue of purity demands a supernatural foundation. This becomes evident when we consider that the morally conscious man who without a religious motive keeps himself pure solely in response to an ethical value, no doubt far transcends the purely natural sphere and adopts an attitude which is the product of spirit, but is not therefore the possessor of purity as a substantial *virtue*. Whereas the purity of the pure-natured—though not, indeed, the product of spirit—is a substantial property of the person, with clearly marked features, the value-response that is unmotivated by religion (as exemplified by the attitude of a conscientious and morally earnest man who regrets the isolation of sex as its own end and the abuse of sex) is no substantial virtue of purity, no quality that really belongs to his being. We cannot describe a morally earnest man (for example, Wilhelm Meister, in his later development, who deliberately combats temptations), nor yet a young man who takes morality seriously (for instance, Tamino in *The Magic Flute*), as possessing the virtue of purity in its strictest sense—the creation of spirit—as we can a Rose of Lima, a Curé d'Ars, or a Stanislaus Kostka. This is a point of the utmost importance for ethics and for psychology also, if we would understand the structure of the spiritual person. The person's conscious spiritual intention is not sufficient in the case of every virtue to construct, as nature can construct, of its own strength a substantial property of his being, with an analogous fullness of content. The properties of the person that are not produced by spirit possess a fullness of content and a substantiality, as characteristics of the entire being which no deliberate moral volition, however victorious, can effect. Purity is, with benevolence, and so on, a marked instance of this. It is only the supernatural union with God and surrender to Him that can give the will of the human spirit power to construct these virtues with a fullness of content, a substantiality, that is not merely analogous, as in the case of the natural virtues, but substantial in a sense incomparably more strict—and as genuine *virtues*, that is to say, habits. In short, only the supernatural reference is sufficient in the case of these virtues to effect a real union between production by the spirit and substantiality.[7]

For the defective substantiality of the former purity cannot be explained as due solely to its incomplete organic possession of the person. Even in the case of a supernaturally motived choice of purity we can distinguish different degrees to which the person is possessed by the virtue. But in the case of the mere idealist a double impotence attaches in principle to the will. In the first place it can never, however successful it may be, effect a substantial transformation of the person in this respect. In the second place, it can never produce the specific quality displayed by the purity of a saint. It is, to be sure, a sufficient foundation for the absence of impurity, and for the qualities of depth, seriousness, and idealism; but purity with its mysterious radiance requires something more, and, as we have already seen, this impotence is sufficiently explained by the fact that the objective value that corresponds to purity, which the pure man has constantly in view, lies beyond its sphere. The value-qualities which the idealist wills in the domain of purity are as remote from the objective value which corresponds to genuine purity as are those which the naturally pure has in view. In this case, no doubt, the fashion in which the value is apprehended and the response given, the quality to which the response is made, is different. The idealist wills before anything else the positive values of which sex may be the subject (in so far as they are intelligible from his naturalist standpoint). He rejects every abuse of sex and wills purity itself as freedom from the corrupting poison of isolated sex,

7. Substantiality, of course, is to be understood here of qualities.

as a certain inviolacy of his spirit's orientation to the ideal, the guarantee that his idealism may take her upward flight unhampered by matter. It is obvious how wide is the gulf which separates purity of this kind from that described above, and still more how the objective correlate of genuine purity represents in contrast something completely new.

The complete spirit-produced virtue of purity is only possible as an element of *Christian* morality, and, even psychologically, presupposes as its objective correlate the new world revealed to us in the countenance of Jesus. Everyone who has an eye for the entirely novel quality of the morality which the saint displays in its splendor will also understand that holiness in every form "radiates" from Jesus the God-man. He will recognize that this morality differs in kind from any merely natural moral perfection, displays an incomparable luster and an incomparable depth, and wins victories no other ethic could achieve. He will see clearly what a gulf divides a noble, temperate, prudent, just, and sincere pagan, a Seneca, for example, or a Socrates, and the Christian in whom baptismal grace has produced its full effect, that is to say, the saint — a St. Paul, for example, or a St. Ambrose. He will understand how the humility which is happy to confess its own nothingness in the presence of God's glory, and will owe nothing to itself, everything to God; the gentleness of the man who, when smitten on the left cheek, turns the right; the love that "supporteth all things, believeth all things, hopeth all things, endureth all things," and which in unreserved self-surrender embraces the meanest, basest, pettiest, most sinful, as the image of God and a soul redeemed for eternal bliss by the merits of Christ's blood and loved by Jesus with an everlasting love; the purity which is the reflected splendor of God's light shining on the soul — how all these are the fruits of an entirely new life in the soul, of kindred essence with the life which beats in the divine-human Heart of Jesus, in whom is the fullness of divine beauty.

And this life — which can derive but from one source, sanctifying grace, not only is in its quality a reflection of Jesus, but presupposes as its objective correlate that picture of God which has been revealed to us in Jesus's teaching, and still more in His being and countenance. For here alone the distinctive quality of this morality is manifest in its *original* source, and it is here, therefore, that our spirit must make contact with it, if it is to be admitted into its sphere. Only the new light which shines here into our spiritual eyes can so reform our nature as to give birth to the perfect virtue of purity. Though there are, no doubt, virtues—justice, for example, truthfulness, and loyalty—which can arise even on the purely natural plane as substantially realized and therefore products of spirit, there rises far above them that glorious world of spirit-born virtues which, in their substantial content and distinctive quality, are possible only as the reflection of the glory which shines upon us from the face of God—the God of whom Jesus said, "Philip, he who hath seen Me hath seen the Father."

(d) Note on the attitude of the pure to art

We may take this opportunity of saying a little about the attitude of the pure man to art and on the question what in art must be regarded as objectively pure or impure. The pure man rejects everything impure, accepts everything pure. But he will have nothing whatever to do with the prudery which scents impurity everywhere. Here, too, it is a matter of discerning the narrow path trodden by those who combine a healthy mistrust of their own nature with freedom of spirit. Just as the right attitude of man on his earthly pilgrimage combines life in fear and trembling with serving the Lord with joy, so here also freedom of spirit and constant watchfulness against everything unclean must go hand in hand.

It is obviously impossible within the limits of this work to discuss the nature of art. We must content ourselves with pointing out as a first principle the peculiar connection which exists between purity and art that is essentially profound—*the art* whose beauty is a reflection of the Godhead. In itself all genuine beauty is, as a genuine objective value, in the widest sense of the term pure. But with its beauty it may combine a sexual appeal. In every department of art there are genuine works of art which possess genuine beauty, but which are at the same time sexually stimulating. This does not necessarily condemn them as impure. At least they are not tainted by sexuality isolated as the object of evil lust, but on the other hand they cannot be termed pure in the strict sense. They are steeped in the dangerous charm of sex and may be a source of temptation. The attitude of the pure man toward works of art of this kind will vary; if he has to struggle against temptation it will be different from what it will be if he is deaf to the siren melody of isolated sex; but above all it will depend on his sensibility to art as such. Either he will see in such works of art only the artistic beauty, and the other aspects will leave him unaffected—though even then his attitude toward them will be marked by a certain distance, and he will never surrender himself to them unreservedly; or he will be conscious of the heated breath of sexual lust in them as a personal danger, in which case he will naturally, as far as possible, avoid all contact with them. But we have in view here, and the point is important, only those works of art in which the sexual appeal is essentially bound up with their artistic quality. The case is entirely different with those works of art which are vehicles of an ultimate transcendent loveliness and greatness, which pours down upon this lower world like the light of the sun: works of art that breathe a sublime beauty which seems to open to us the gate of heaven. Such beauty is at the opposite pole to everything paltry and impure. Not only is it pure in itself like the Beauty of which it is the reflection; it is also specifically purifying, and contributes more than almost any other agent to free the heart from the intoxicating poison of sex isolated as its own end. It raises a man above this sphere, touches and expands the soul, arouses a longing for its heavenly home, emancipates it and guides it into the deepest region of its own interior, and enkindles in our heart a burning desire for God, the everlasting Beauty, and Jesus, "fairest of the sons of men."

Wherever this beauty speaks to us from a work of art the fact that the mere subject matter contains something which in itself might be a cause of temptation, for example, the naked body, is of no significance whatever. This beauty silences the siren strain which otherwise might proceed from the purely material factor, the subject treated. Such works of art can never be dangerous to men capable of appreciating art. The pure man, if only he is sensitive to art, will never find in them anything which could harm him or forbid him to surrender himself to their beauty. This, of course, is not to deny that to an inartistic man even these sublime works of art, in themselves specifically pure, might prove dangerous, if he were at the same time particularly susceptible to temptations of this kind. But in this sense even Holy Scripture can be dangerous, since it speaks frankly about many things which might prove the occasion of temptations to a reader whose attitude was mistaken.

In view of these dangers we are obliged, no doubt, to take practical measures, especially in the field of education, but we are in no way justified in condemning as impure any product of this essentially sincere and sublime art merely because sex enters into its subject matter.

In this connection we often meet with a deplorable prudery and judgments passed in accordance with totally inadequate standards. People fail to recognize the existence of a pseudo-art which is impure through and through, even though its subject matter may have nothing whatever to do with sex. And, on the other hand, works of art which are steeped in that quintessential beauty of which we have spoken are judged impure simply because they represent, for example, a nude figure, or because the existence of sex is in one form or another brought to our notice. But, on the other hand, we must emphatically insist that there is a contemporary pseudo-art that is not entitled to plead, in excuse of its profound impurity, that the sexual danger has been removed by its specifically technical excellence. Its predilection for sexually dangerous subjects proceeds from a genuinely impure attitude. Its nude figures, particularly in "realist" art, produce an "exhibitionist" effect, and this unpleasant character is often artificially emphasized by partial clothing. But this particular pseudo-art, be it remembered, is primarily impure in its spirit, and thus makes its nudes impure; its impurity does not consist in the mere fact that it depicts the nude.[8] Art of this kind is still unhealthy and unclean, even when it does not represent the human body—the impurity is due to the absence of any genuine art.

The campaign, in itself most necessary, against the repulsive immod-

8. See also the excellent remarks of Franz Walter in his "Der Leib und sein Recht im Christentum" (The Body and Its Rights in Christianity) (Donauwörth, 1910), part 2, chap. 2, especially pp. 49 4‾95.

esty which meets us in every department of contemporary culture may very easily, if it is conducted by the inartistic, be misled into seeing impurity where it does not exist and objecting to the treatment of anything which in any way involves sex. Those who adopt such a canon will condemn as impure even sublime and pure works of art simply because for the inartistic their subject might possess a sexual appeal. But the spirit which inspires a judgment of this kind is wholly uncatholic, particularly when, as is not seldom the case, it is united with prudery. It is diametrically opposed to the breadth, magnanimity, and classical sincerity which distinguish the Church.[9] We breathe here a confined moral atmosphere which prevents us seeing things *in conspectu Dei* (in the sight of God). What is really in accord with the spirit of the Church is most easily discovered from the liturgy, her sublime voice. There we find no insincere attempt to deny the existence of sex, no prudish suppression, no timid cloaking. On the contrary, we find that sincerity which is a fundamental constituent of purity, that clearness of vision which does not deny the existence of sex but openly grapples with it and by so doing remains wholly untainted by its intoxicating breath and raises us above it. What so pure as the voice of the Church? Yet does it not speak plainly and openly on every topic, from the Ave Maria and the Compline hymn to the sublime Gospel of the Annunciation? Indeed, we have only to remember the words of the purest of the pure, the blessed Virgin Mary: "How shall this be, seeing I know not man?"

9. Ibid., part 1, chap. 2, iii, pp. 157-58.

CHAPTER SEVEN

The Intrinsic Dangers of Sex

HOW THEN does the pure man, who possesses purity in that highest form which we have described, behave in the actual exercise of sex? What inner attitude does he adopt which ennobles the act of marriage and outweighs all the dangers incident to this sphere? This is a question with which we are already familiar. But before answering it we must study the dangers inherent in sex as such, and not only in its abuse. Apart from the three aspects which we have already learned to recognize, sex is further distinguished by three factors which involve a special danger for the person as a spiritual being. The sexual act is in a certain sense the central act of the body. It is, in a sense, the awakening of the corporeal nature, otherwise asleep; it represents the most vital and most intense experience of which the body is capable — is, we may say, the sole experience in which it is brought into act as a whole. In it the vital nature lays bare, so to speak, its deepest roots.[1] Sex further represents the greatest power within

1. This phenomenon naturally stands in close organic connection with the extraordinariness of sex on the one hand, and on the other with the fact that the act of marriage produces new life. In speaking of the sleep and awakening of the corporeal nature we have in mind, not its disappearance

the vital-corporeal sphere, not indeed as an irresistible force like sickness or the need of food, but in its distinctive quality and structural position within the person.

The orgasm in its violence, its fury, its convulsion, has a tendency to overpower the spirit. In the sexual act the spirit is exposed as on no other occasion to the danger of being "swamped" by the vital nature, and that for a double reason. In the first place because, as a result of the close and profound union between the body and the spiritual soul, this physical experience, the most profound of all except death,[2] tends to drag the spirit wholly into its domain. If on the one hand the spirit soars above the corporeal nature, on the other hand it is at the same time in a special fashion sunk in the body and enveloped by it. The sexual experience strives, as it were, to pull the spirit down from its eminence and make it the complete prisoner of the body. This is, of course, only a tendency which physically can never attain its goal. For the sovereignty of the immortal soul over the corporeal-vital nature cannot be substantially destroyed by any behavior of the spiritual person. But a moral absorption is always involved in the sexual act, unless the spirit is at the same time brought into action in a fashion correspondingly profound, and the due proportion thus restored between the spiritual and the vital-corporeal natures, a proportion which of course implies the supremacy of the former. From this point of view, therefore, sex is something which is not dangerous *only* when abused, but involves for fallen man an intrinsic danger which must be compensated by a particular attitude of the spirit. We shall see a little later in what alone this compensation can consist.

But from yet another point of view the spiritual person is in danger of

from or emergence into consciousness, but a metaphysical characteristic which it displays by comparison with the spiritual nature—whereas the material nature must be pronounced in its turn asleep in comparison with the vital-corporeal. The orgasm is the actuation of the vital-corporeal nature in which it attains the maximum intensity of which it is capable, and in the mere quality of its being approaches the spiritual most closely. Obviously the term "actuation" is not used here in the strict sense of the term, but in an analogous and more qualitative sense.

2. Death is the greatest disactuation of the body—therefore, in one respect the opposite of the orgasm. On the other hand, the exposure of the roots and the "depth" of the corporeal event common, though in a totally different fashion, to both (as also to very great physical suffering, for example, the pangs of childbirth), constitutes a certain affinity between them.

being "swamped" by the orgasm. There is a peculiar giving up of one's self-possession which may occur in the most diverse departments of the emotional life. Let us consider first the more general form of self-loss. A man is suddenly seized with panic, and flies, mad with terror. He has, as we say, "lost his head." An experience of this kind is, in fact, an avulsion, in which a man loses control of himself, and is passively borne away by the current of his emotion. Even that moral self-possession which enters into every action fully deserving the name is for the moment lost. Strictly speaking, there is no longer any choice. The subject cannot be truly said to assent to his action. Every passion which overpowers me and carries me away or washes me overboard—as contrasted with my conduct when I deliberately throw myself into it—represents such a loss of self, that I am passively drawn under by the waves. It is the exact opposite of the case when a man surrenders to a value which takes possession of him—for instance, when he is profoundly affected by the consideration of God's goodness or is seized with an overpowering sorrow for his sins. For this experience of being seized, taken possession of, which is preeminently characteristic of religious experiences and, above all, of mystical states in which the person is raised out of and above himself, is distinguished precisely by the assent of the central spiritual self which it implies. There is, therefore, in spite of the apparent analogy between the two kinds of experience, no loss of self-possession. On the contrary, it is in these experiences which involve the profoundest depths of our personality that we are most our own, because we belong *more* to God, "who is more present to us than we are to ourselves." The assent which in ordinary circumstances we must expressly give to an experience is here given by the Object which possesses us—it is implicit in our possession by It. Thus the specifically unsanctioned loss of self, the being carried away, and the implicitly sanctioned possession are the greatest conceivable opposites.

There is, however, a giving up of our self-possession which answers even more fully to the description, when a man is not simply carried away by a passion in spite of his reason, but, so to speak, flings himself away. For example, a man flies into a violent passion. But he still keeps control of himself. Suddenly his rage takes such hold of him that he, as it were, throws the reins to it, and places himself unreservedly at its disposal. In an act of insane presumption he stakes everything on one throw and casts himself away as a whole. This psychological state at its purest finds formal expression in the attitude of the man who curses from rage, in the unsanctioned oath—the curse in the strict and original meaning of the word. "If I cannot have this, I will be lost forever"—is the verbal utterance of what here passes in the soul. This flinging oneself away represents a specific attitude which our ancestors understood far better than we. We have but to remember the legend of the Flying Dutchman, in which a typical flinging oneself away of the kind we are describing meets with so terrible a punishment, or of the cases in which a man delivered his soul to the devil simply in order to obtain a particular thing he wanted there and then. This giving oneself away as a whole, which, be it only for a moment, subverts the entire order inherent in the constitution of our nature and the objective hierarchy of goods and values, above all destroys our life for and in the presence of God, admits, of course, differences of degree. Something of this kind may happen inwardly without involving such an explicit self-abandonment at one decisive point. But in that case the offender feels later an unmistakable sense of guilt, feels that though his act was not fully conscious he has wantonly broken loose from the order established by God, and the self-possession which that order demanded has yielded to a self-abandonment. He has, so he feels, in a certain sense, flung away his existence and must have fallen irretrievably into the abyss, if God's mercy, operative already in the *possibility* of retracing his steps, had not held him back.

It is already evident that the peculiar *hubris* that this universal flinging away of self under the influence of some passion implies, represents something *completely new* and distinctive, as compared with that self-loss of which we have already spoken, which is involved when we are carried away illegitimately. It can assume the most varied guises. But something of the kind is in a distinctive fashion contained *objectively* in the full realization of sex. That experience involves an abandonment of the entire person, which always constitutes a casting away of oneself in the sense explained above, a departure from the divinely established order, if it is not expressly introduced into that inner order by a spiritual experience even more potent and, moreover, wholly anchored in God, which transforms it into a legitimately sanctioned expression.[3] The realization of sex is always a flinging away of self, when it is not a divinely sanctioned surrender of self. Hence this second factor also requires a particular spiritual attitude to counterbalance it, in virtue of which this casting away of the self becomes a legitimate possession which in no way disturbs the inner order.

And, finally, we must call attention to the fact that certain features of sex, independently of its three possible aspects, possess from the purely external standpoint an ugliness which represents in this domain the fault which runs through every stratum of fallen humanity. Like the corruption of the body after death, there are many things in life which are visible effects of the Fall. From these sex and the marriage act are not exempt. A certain nucleus of vital brutality which in some way conflicts with the excellence and nobility of the spirit is objectively bound up with certain features of sex. When the marriage act is performed in the highest and purest fashion these features are suppressed. Love then dominates the situation so completely that they are totally unable to find expression. But they are merely unexpressed, not objectively transformed into something else, as are all those other features which we have just discussed. Here the compensation consists in complete repression. The moment the sexual act is not viewed from within, in its divinely ordained function, but appears in its external aspect, the stark vital brutality, the ugliness of certain features, makes itself powerfully felt. It is, moreover, this aspect of sex which inspires a peculiar shrinking from it, a certain withdrawal of

3. To yield to any sexual temptation, be it simply by admitting a sinful thought, is to be carried away. But only the complete realization of sex, that is to say, the orgasm, involves this flinging away of one's self which, moreover, is objectively present in the psychological aspect of the event. It is no question here of the failure to resist temptation, the typical case of being borne away by the current. On the contrary, the objective bodily event as such, altogether apart from the spiritual attitude of the subject, involves a complete self-abandonment of the person, a casting away of self as a whole, which simply on that account stands in need of a deliberate act of the spirit to transform it. There is a factor at work here which is not brought into being by any sinful attitude of the soul, but is objectively present in the sexual act as such, and always comes into operation, if it is not checked by a special attitude of the soul which counterbalances it.

the spirit from the brutality of the vital sphere, which, in its external aspect, contains an element of animality.[4] This shrinking from the brutal aspects of sex, which, moreover, is an essential factor of modesty, is legitimately set aside only when we are, so to speak, conscious of a vocation to enter this domain, whether in wedded love, which, as we have already pointed out, causes the external aspect to disappear automatically, or in nursing the sick, in which the external aspect of sex is deprived of ugliness by love of our neighbor, and the entire situation transformed by its background of sickness, or, again, as a doctor, when the external aspect not only remains, but is emphasized so exclusively that it is neutralized by a completely detached scientific attitude. We must, however, insist that this shrinking from the brutal is totally different from the reverent awe which shrinks from violating the mystery and the intimacy of sex. This reverent awe constitutes the far nobler, more important and more spiritual factor in the feeling of modesty.

4. Hence, every form of sexual instruction that reveals sex too nakedly and treats it too objectively offends our sense of modesty because it takes no account of this shyness.

CHAPTER EIGHT

The Reformation of Sex
Effected by Wedded Love

WHAT ATTITUDE, what act, then, possesses the power to unite sex organically with the spiritual person, transform it, and take from it everything which could dim the clear shining of the soul before God? *Love* alone can thus ennoble sex. And, further, not love of any kind, but love of an altogether distinctive quality, a love that bears the formally affixed seal of the lovers' assent, and which issues in a special act of a social character. In its quality this love must be wedded love. The *intentio unitiva* (purpose of uniting) contained in all love acquires in the love peculiar to marriage an entirely new function, unitive in the fullest sense; it becomes the leitmotif of this relationship. In contrast to the typical friendship, in which the pursuit of a common object, community of tastes, views, and so on, constitutes the leitmotif, the other person is here strictly speaking the object. Each is wholly for the other, and mutual love the burden of the song. Thus the *intentio unitiva* inherent in every love attains a wholly different significance. Either party seeks to share in the *being* of the other, not simply in his or her life and thoughts. There is, further, the specific mutual completion which this unitive tendency effects in the case of man and wife. And, finally, there is the special way of "being in love," in the noblest sense of that expression, which puts a specific stamp upon wedded love, that peculiar and most intense receptivity for which the entire charm of the other nature, in its unique individuality, not only unfolds itself to our delighted vision, but, in a fashion elsewhere unparalleled, holds us captive.

In the second place, the only love which can transform sex is essentially a love solemnly sanctioned by the person himself. It cannot just exist. The free spiritual core of our personality must expressly approve it, must, so to speak, declare its full assent, must explicitly cooperate in its unitive tendency. The *intentio unitiva* must thus become a serious choice of the will to belong perpetually to the other. It must express itself in the social act of self-delivery to the other for the whole of life, and be permanently embodied in the objective bond which that act creates. And this surrender, this solemn binding of oneself to another for life, must take place in the sight of God (*in conspectu Dei*). God must, so to speak, be the owner of the bond.

Only wedded love in this, its most perfect form, as a special kind of love and as love in wedlock, is able to transform the act of wedded union from within and make it truly pure. How then is this transformation effected, and why is this love alone capable of accomplishing it? Love alone, as the most fruitful and most intense act, the act which brings the entire spirit into operation, possesses the requisite power to transform thoroughly the entire qualitative texture of an experience. The will, the informing power in the sphere of conduct, can, as it were, grasp our emotional experiences only from the outside. It can—indeed for this its assent is sufficient—*liberate* the person from an experience; can, for instance, render his envy up to a certain point harmless, can "behead" it, or immure it within the person; but it cannot destroy it, as love destroys it. By his will the person can, so to speak, overleap his emotional life with a magnificent gesture, but he cannot change its quality. Hence the will by itself can never effect an organic union between sex on the one hand and the heart and mind on the other. Whatever the aim the will sets before itself, so long as the act of marriage is motived by the will alone, it remains a foreign body within the life of the spirit, and though possibly free from sin, it remains, nevertheless, something without organic connection with the life of the person, its brutal aggressor, something which simply coexists with the heart and the mind and therefore retains a certain animality. As we have already seen, the mere relation to an end can never impart an inner significance to the act of marriage as an experience, still less ennoble it. Love, on the other hand, can wholly dissolve any experience and transform the quality of its texture; in more technical language, can strip its *matter* of the old *form* and invest it with a new. Here, however, it has to deal with a domain which is especially coordinated with it as wedded love.

As we have seen, the significance of sex consists in its being the specific sphere in which wedded love finds expression and fulfillment. Love alone is therefore in a position to unite sex organically with the heart and mind. Wedded love alone holds, so to speak, the key which by realizing it can unlock the significance of sex as an experience and reveal to the person its true positive aspect. In contrast with the bare will it can inwardly link the act of wedded union with the person, since that act represents its specific expression and fulfillment. Inasmuch as it is *wedded* love it can incorporate organically the act of married union into the life of the person. Inasmuch as it is *love* it can specifically ennoble it. And inasmuch as it is both it can fully counterbalance the double danger of "swamping" described above. This is, on the contrary, quite beyond the power of the bare will.

We will first consider the danger of foundering in the vital-corporeal, of "drowning." As always, the person's good intention suffices to save him from guilt. The good intention, not to be "swamped," or swallowed up, is thus by itself able to exclude all moral fault when the act of wedded union is a duty. But it is not capable by itself of preventing the actual drowning, so that a submersion is changed into a seizure. Love alone, as the most intense, most central act of the spirit, is capable of this. Love alone represents an activity, an actualization, of the spiritual person so central and intensely conscious through and through that it keeps up with the supreme activity or actuation of the body in the act of wedlock.

Hence, love alone can even at this moment maintain the sovereignty of the spirit over the body. It owes this power primarily to the fact that in its specific character as wedded love it can enter into an inner and organic relation with sex. It does not therefore act as a force which remains outside the physical event and conquers it from without, as when, for instance, a man remains spiritually untouched by severe bodily pain, but makes the physical event an expression of itself. And this it is able to do partly in virtue of the intrinsic correspondence between them, because the physical act possesses the capacity to become the expression of love, but still more in virtue of its intrinsic strength, as the most intense, profound and all-embracing activity or actuation of the spirit, in which the spirit realizes most triumphantly its sovereignty over the entire vital-corporeal domain.

Wedded love, however, can perform this function only when it is consciously and deliberately anchored in God—is a love in God. Only when the spirit cleaves to God by an express act can it keep its head above the waves of animal life which at this moment break violently upon it. This factor—conscious anchorage in God—is precisely that which turns the scale in favor of the spirit so that the danger is fully outweighed. And with this anchorage is bound up the conviction that only with God's express sanction may sex be brought into act. Only when the person, knowing that God expressly sanctions its exercise, yields himself to his partner in the most active and self-conscious wedded love, and, moreover, by a special act deliberately attaches himself to God, is he able to transform the act which represents the supreme activity or actuation of the body in its entire texture as an experience; that is to say, to invest its matter with a new form, render it subservient to the spirit, deprive it of its independence and remain throughout its accomplishment unalterably in the Divine Presence.

The same is true of the second kind of "drowning"—the abandonment of the possession of self, the casting oneself away. The bare will is indeed able to prevent this element of the sexual act, the casting away of self which it always involves, from invading the spiritual and moral attitude, and it can exercise this power even in the absence of wedded love;

for example, when a husband gives himself up to his wife because he feels it his duty as a husband to do so. Indeed, a solemn decision of the will anchored in God can even invest with its sanction this casting away of self inherent in the sexual act and give it the objective significance of a surrender. But no actual transformation is thereby effected to turn the casting away of self by a change of quality into an actual self-surrender, and really transform sex as an experience, for it is this aspect which in this connection is of decisive importance. Here, too, it is only from outside that the will can impress its stamp. Here, too, it is love alone which can really inform the matter of sex—that is, the specific wedded love for which the act of married union is the appointed expression. By its operation the factor of complete self-abandonment objectively contained in the orgasm is totally changed; remolded, so to speak, from a casting away of self into a self-surrender whereby the sexual act really becomes throughout a fulfillment of wedded love's *intentio unitiva.* That love becomes its soul, so that everything about it is now its expression and fulfillment, and the factor of self-abandonment is transformed into a unique self-surrender whose sanction issues from the profoundest depths of the person—so that in every respect the marriage act is an adequate and intrinsically significant expression, in which the person does not lose himself, does not, on the strength of a passing impulse, wantonly fling himself away as a whole, but makes a solemn donation of himself to his partner once for all and for life.

But, as wedded love cannot by itself counterbalance the danger of "swamping," so by itself it is insufficient to preserve the inner order during the act of sex and maintain the possession of self. Only when the person remains in God, affirming his adherence to God by an explicit act, does the supreme surrender to a creature not involve "letting oneself go." For a genuine self-possession subsists only so long as a man remains in God. Wedded love itself may become a casting away of self of a far deeper nature, if God be forgotten for the beloved—as soon, indeed, as an act of unreserved surrender to the beloved is accomplished outside Him. It is to God alone that we may, in the full sense, surrender ourselves without reserve, or can do so without losing ourselves. Then,

indeed, then only, it is true that "whosoever loseth his soul shall find it."
In God, however, man may surrender himself even to a fellow creature.
But this surrender must be really incorporated into the surrender to God
and must in turn be intrinsically "formed" by the latter. Thus and thus
alone do we get rid of all caprice and levity, all staking everything on the
moment, every breach of the objective order of values, and interior disorder. For only while man abides in God does he leave everything in its
right place. The moment we are no longer first and foremost servants of
God, and do not, at least habitually, choose Him above all things, the
inner order is already destroyed, and even instinctively we shun His presence. This is true in a very special sense of the marriage act, with its
strong emotional convulsion, tensest drama, and supreme surrender. It is
now that anchorage in God must be realized effectively, if the disorder
above described is not to supervene and make it impossible to remain
before His face. For this new "forming," this "reformation" of the marriage act, already in some measure effected when it is made the expression of wedded love and union, this actual adherence to God, is
produced precisely by the consciousness that it is only with God's
express sanction we are entering the sexual domain, by a special glance
directed to Him, and by a reverent awe of sex which never permits love's
unreserved surrender to the other to become an unrestrained self-indul-
gence, but imparts to it for the first time the character of a union of love
issuing organically from the inmost center of the person and invested
with his formal assent.

It is also, as we have already remarked, only wedded love that can
remove completely, for experience at least, the ugly aspect attaching to
certain constituents of the marriage act. Love alone enables us so to view
everything from within and so to dominate the situation that this aspect
is no longer experienced. Love alone possesses the power to regard everything in its highest significance, and to see everything belonging to the
other person ensouled by the charm of his or her nature and spirit, so that
the factor of brutal vitality is buried, not only for *thought*, but for *experience*. And in this case also it is the reverent knowledge that it is by God's
express permission that we have crossed the frontiers of sex, which gives

the soul that humble freedom, that conscious emancipation, by which we accept the fact of sex as it is, and ennoble it by the penetrating vision of love, undisturbed by the fact that here too the results of the Fall make themselves felt. In relation to these results of the Fall we may apply, *mutatis mutandis*, to the wedded love that is anchored fast in God what was written of supernatural love in relation to sin generally: "Love covereth a multitude of sins."

CHAPTER NINE

Recapitulation: The Ideal of Wedded Purity

As we have pointed out already, the specific positive value for whose realization sex in its ultimate significance is ordained is not purity, but the love which gives and sacrifices self in the most profound and mysterious union. If, however, we would remain completely and perfectly pure in the exercise of sex, we must realize in our use of it just these values of self-devoting love and mysterious union. Only so does the act of marriage really become something wholly pure; indeed, a special occasion of exercising the virtue of purity. How then must the truly pure man experience sex, so that he need not depart an instant from the Divine Presence, but may continue to shine with undimmed radiance before God? In asking the question we are primarily enquiring how the nature of wedded purity *positively displays itself,* and shall study in detail the qualities it manifests. The standpoint which has governed our treatment hitherto—the question, namely, what specific factors are required to compensate for the dangers inherent in the act of marriage—is relegated to the background.

In this connection we must distinguish different degrees of purity. There are men who possess a deep-rooted will to purity but are by nature impure. Not only do they suffer from individual temptations, which, so to speak, assail them from without: the entire bent of their nature is toward sex, the charm of sex isolated as its own end. Nevertheless, their will can firmly choose purity, and they can avoid every deliberate surrender to impurity. But the will has not yet attained that organic supremacy within the entire person which effects a remolding of the nature as a whole. Such a man has not reached the point when his heart is emancipated from the sphere of evil lust, and is, on the contrary, distressed and depressed by anything impure, and when his thoughts dwell in a region remote from the domain of sexual charm loved for its own sake. He has attained only the first degree of purity. His actions are pure and his will is pure, but his *nature* is not yet pure. The virtue of purity in the strict sense does not yet belong to it. An incomparably higher degree of purity is represented by the man in whose nature the will to purity has become organic. His thoughts and desires are not occupied with the attractions of sex as an independent sphere, neither with the quality of evil lust nor with the specific fascination of sex. In situations which present any danger of this kind he shuns it from the outset; he never seeks it nor rejoices at its presence. To be sure, on occasion he may feel the force of temptation, may, no doubt, be naturally susceptible to the siren melody of isolated sex. But the profound rejection of everything impure has become so much a part of his psychological organization that not only his conduct and his will, but his entire emotional life has become pure. Apart from isolated temptations which are of an exceptional character, his nature has become such that impurity, wherever he meets it—that is to say, sex in isolation— inspires him with disgust and sorrow, that he avoids everything which emits the oppressive intoxicating breath of fleshly lust, and his thoughts do not normally turn in that direction. Such an attitude displays the perfect virtue of purity, even if sensibility to isolated sex is not wholly absent.

There is finally a type of purity which is crowned with a peculiar aureole.[1] There are men on whom God has bestowed this special grace:

---

1. The degrees of purity here described, particularly that depicted as the ideal, are viewed from the standpoint of wedded purity. We are attempting to depict the ideal of purity in the exercise of sex. And in this connection we must remember that ideal purity is here bound up with the ideal wedded

although in the highest degree sensitive to the positive aspect of sex, they are insensitive to its isolated fascination and still more to evil lust. God has bound so closely their sensibility to sex with the capacity of love that it is only in the service of a perfect wedded love that sex possesses any appeal and is aroused in them. Beyond all others, persons of this kind walk unspotted in the midst of a sinful world. The breath of impurity can never be even a source of *temptation*. But this is not in the least a matter of temperament. The sensibility of such men to sex is no doubt temperamental. But that sex can speak to them only when accompanied by an entire and profound love and the knowledge of God's approval, so that temptations are thus excluded altogether, is no quality of temperament, but a grace—though certainly a grace which requires the cooperation of free will. Only if the person deliberately *wills* what is pure and rejects everything impure, clearly understanding its negative character, can he preserve this grace. Should he relax this cooperation, and turn away from God, the sphere of self-contained sexual fascination will soon begin to speak to him, if not also that of evil lust. For the law of the flesh dwells in every man, and if he is not temperamentally insensitive to sex, this purity can be preserved only by a will that with unrelenting fidelity follows in the footsteps of grace.[2] It is upon this last and supreme type that we shall base our account of the ideal of wedded purity.

When we try to determine the attitude in wedlock of a man of this type we find that its primary and most distinctive characteristic is the fact that in his marriage relationship sex appeals to him only by its tender intimacy, its touching surrender, its mysterious power to unite and fuse, that, though a source of profound joy, it is not in the narrower sense sensually attractive, and has none of the oppressive fumes of evil lust. This does not exclude the presence of a purely physical inclination and attraction to sex, but the physical aspect of sex can only affect the soul as the

union. That is to say, though the value of tender and complete surrender and union of love represent, as we have already seen, something distinct from purity, nevertheless, wedded purity unfolds its fairest blossoms and strikes its deepest root where the special values which belong to the wedded union in its highest form are most completely realized.

2. This third and supreme type of wedded purity is a specially convincing proof that the genuine virtue of purity, as contrasted with natural purity, essentially requires a supernatural motive, and can be produced only with supernatural aid.

subject of the qualities just mentioned. The profound reverence of the pure, his shrinking from all direct contemplation of sex, and his deep understanding of its function, as the means through which wedded love finds its fulfillment, never allow him to make the physical pleasure as such his object. The pure man therefore experiences, as no other, the depth, the seriousness, the power to unite fundamentally, and the extraordinary character of the marriage act. For him it is no mere accessory of marriage, but something invested with profound significance and the source of profound happiness. This, of course, supposes an ideal marriage, in which both partners love each other from the depths of their being, are kept in mental contact by a complete understanding, and see each other, so to speak, by a mutual indwelling of their souls. When the physical expression is no longer fundamentally adequate, because the spiritual unity is no longer absolute, it loses more and more its power to give joy, until in the unhappy marriage it has become a burdensome duty.

To understand, however, the ennoblement of sex for the pure we must briefly examine the part played by tenderness. It is a factor of no slight importance. For that specific wedded love which, as we have seen, must pervade the entire sexual relationship is avowedly tender.

The better to understand the ennobling operation of the spirit of tenderness in the domain of sex, that is to say, in relation to the marriage act, we must consider shortly its nature.[3] Tenderness by no means coincides with sex, but occupies a distinct domain of its own. In the first place, as contrasted with sexuality, it organically attaches to every form of love which attains a certain quality. It has no independent existence, but is essentially a *consequence* and special *expression of love*. It is distinguished by a freedom from constraint, a kindheartedness, a gentleness. It is a special form of love's free outflowing which reaches the other. It is a softness of love's melting, but serene, bright, and free as love itself.

Every genuine love contains two fundamental elements which may be termed respectively *intentio unitiva* (will to unity) and *benevolentia* (desire for the good of the beloved). The distinctive response to value which every genuine love represents, inasmuch as in such love we reply to the values perceived in the other person with a response of a wholly indi-

---

3. It has obviously nothing to do with what is often incorrectly called tenderness—that specific craving to snuggle up to another which quite unconsciously seeks contact with some other living being.

vidual quality, contains just these two constituents. Our response is on the one hand a lavish generosity which makes another being its object and wills that being: we lavish upon him or her our affection and goodwill. This element is displayed most perfectly when we will the salvation of the beloved. But our response is at the same time a will to union, an *intentio unitiva*, the longing to be united with the other, the gift of our heart to him, or her, the will to belong to him, to be one with him, to share his being. And this response, too, is throughout the response to a perceived value. Indeed, it is even more specifically a value-response than lavish generosity; it is more exclusively motived and supported by a value, whereas generosity is, by comparison, more spontaneous and represents rather a full *unfolding* of the humbly and reverently loving ego within ourselves than a specific *response to value*. All love, indeed, necessarily contains both factors in mutual penetration, but according to the nature of the love either may predominate. In the love of God the *intentio unitiva* is the dominant factor; in love of one's neighbor, generous and affectionate goodwill. In mother-love *benevolentia* is supreme; in the love of husband and wife the *intentio unitiva*. But no act can be truly *love* unless both factors are somehow present. The passionate craving which seeks to possess the other has no right to the name of love. It lacks both *benevolentia* and *intentio unitiva*. For the craving to possess is no genuine desire for union, since in this case it is not a possession of the other's heart which is desired, a possession which cannot exist unless the beloved possess in turn the heart of the lover, but the ownership of the beloved as a chattel. The moment a real *intentio unitiva* is added to the desire, the latter is combined with a real love. But then the factor of *benevolentia* is always present as well.

Tenderness as a disposition is a particular development of that love, in which the attitude of *benevolentia* in a certain sense prevails. The lover desires to effect a union of a special kind with the beloved by employing the material of his generous love; he seeks to clothe and envelop her with this material, his affectionate goodwill. This communication of lavish affection is, it is true, of secondary importance in the lover's eyes as compared with his ultimate intention, the beloved's happiness in time and eternity. The external tokens of tenderness, effects of this tender disposition, caressing and embracing, are essentially a by-product. They can never become the essential, nor even represent the ideal, method of communicating this generous affection. But, on the other hand, they are a much more unambiguous and immediate road to it than any number of services rendered. For they represent no practical benefit to be conferred upon the beloved, but only my love itself. If I make anyone a present or help in need, love is not in the same way the substance of the entire proceeding as if I caress or embrace that person.

All the external tokens of tenderness are not to an equal degree a precipitate of the tender disposition; that is to say, they are not all primary means of transmitting that material of generous affection inherent in love. The kiss, which may be regarded as the center and crown of the external tokens of tenderness, is principally an expression or, more truly, a fulfillment of the *intentio unitiva*. But it is its fulfillment for every species of love—not only for wedded love. It plays this part in parents' love for their child, in the child's for parents, in the love of friend for friend.[4] It is, indeed, the fulfillment and expression of the highest love for one's neighbor. St. Francis kissed the lepers because in him a supreme love revealed itself which overcame his natural disgust. This function of the kiss as the expression of love toward one's neighbor is clearly seen in the liturgical kiss of peace, and the highest love of which a creature is capable—love of Jesus, God and man—craves the kiss. We kiss His wounds; and holy Church exclaims: "Let Him kiss me with the kisses of His mouth!" Naturally, the kiss possesses a quite different character according to the kind of love it serves to express. But it is always a special expression of love, as signifying that spiritual contact between two persons which love as such involves. It expresses a gaze of each into the other, that incomparable entrance into the personality of another which love represents.

4. English and American readers must remember that on the Continent the kiss is the regular greeting of friendship between men as well as women. In Japan, on the other hand, the kiss is confined to parents and little children. In reading this paragraph the important part played by social convention should not be forgotten. [Trans.]

We must therefore beware of confusing the external signs of tenderness with its specific disposition. They possess, as we have seen, a double significance—as media by which the material of generous affection is transmitted in a distinctive fashion, and as a fulfillment of the *intentio unitiva*. Certain gestures of tenderness, the kiss, for instance, primarily subserve the union; others, for example, the caress, primarily transmit generous affection. But the tender disposition is always characterized principally by the direct transmission of affectionate goodwill.

If, therefore, there is to be tenderness, several factors are essential. In the first place the factor of *benevolentia* must not be weak, and secondly the relation between the parties must be of such a kind that the love itself is its leitmotif. Of such a relationship wedded love is the typical example. Moreover, this second factor is here of the utmost importance for two reasons. In the first place, because only a relationship of which love is the leitmotif brings with it the need to transmit directly the material of affectionate goodwill. In those forms of love in which *benevolentia* predominates, but of which love is not the leitmotif—love of one's neighbor, for example—the goodwill expresses itself primarily in acts of service. Only when love plays the leading role in a relationship is there the need for a direct transmission of the material of *benevolentia*. And, in the second place in this case alone is there that dwelling with the object of love and that entrance into the sanctum of his personality which tenderness distinctly involves. For tenderness urges me, as it were, to envelop in loving kindness every feature of the beloved's being to the minutest recess of his personality. I seek, not simply to capture by generous affection the most central nucleus of his personality, but, so to speak, to follow lovingly all the outlines of another's nature. I desire, as it were, to fuse myself with his essential form, and repeat the acts in which his spirit expresses itself. I am fain to catch and cherish the fragrance of a being different from my own, the breath and luster of his personality. All this is possible only if love plays the leading part throughout.

To sum up the results of our inquiry hitherto: tender love exists whenever the *intentio unitiva* occupies the foreground or—which amounts to the same thing—where love is the specific leitmotif, but only when a high degree of *benevolentia* is also present. The distinctive disposition of tenderness is materially constituted by *benevolentia*, but obviously presupposes an active *intentio unitiva*. The *intentio unitiva* manifests the aim of direct transmission, the *benevolentia* determines the quality of what is transmitted. The more weakly the factor of *benevolentia* is developed, the *intentio unitiva* remaining unaltered, the less tender the love. A love between husband and wife, for example, in which *benevolentia* is less developed will not possess the character of tenderness so fully as one in which *benevolentia* plays a more important part. The kinder and softer and more refined a love, if it expressly craves union with the beloved, the tenderer it is.

But the tenderness or otherwise of a man further depends — this factor is also of decisive importance — on the degree to which he possesses an expansive nature which demands expression, and how far he is free from repressions. Tender men are men who, besides a great capacity for love, possess a general trait of soft and refined delicacy and sensitiveness, and in whom the organic penetration of the body by the soul is particularly close. Those distinctively material, insensitive men whose bodies, like a ponderous dead mass, weigh heavy on the soul are never tender. Language itself witnesses to the connection between physical and psychological tenderness. Nor is there anything passionate or fierce about tenderness; it is, on the contrary, warm, kind-hearted, and mild.

This specific disposition we call tenderness has an important function to perform in the married union. For the pure tenderness, this unconstrained transmission to the other of the material of generous affection, will permeate the entire act of marriage. Tenderness in its specific quality, free from passion, refined, responsive, and even, brings out in special relief the fusion which marriage effects. It is an element in that transfiguring glory which dispels every shadow from the act of wedded union. The bright beam of genuine tenderness which altogether transcends the vital sphere and in which the spirit is wholly supreme, retains indeed complete mastery of itself, penetrates every dark place and invests the entire proceeding with an untroubled peace. With the pure, tenderness has got the start of sexual desire. The marriage union must be penetrated and permeated by tenderness; must, indeed, be experienced as the unique climax of tenderness.

But we must not therefore conclude that the ideal of wedded purity admits only tenderness, to the exclusion of sexual desire. Since, as we have often insisted already, the two must go hand in hand, and, moreover, it is sexual desire which makes possible the unique intimacy, the mysterious profundity, and the objective bond of the marriage act, its presence constitutes a distinctive value. The unique character of this ultimate union, its mystery, its extraordinariness, its ecstasy, its intimacy—all these elements—unintelligible to the man who is simply tender but insensitive to sex—belong to the ideal experience of sex. But tenderness must enjoy a certain supremacy and permeate the married union with its unfettered affection. It is, moreover, a factor which plays a decisive part in counteracting the danger inherent in the act of marriage.

But for the pure the act of self-donation is before everything else accompanied by a special reference to God. I have already pointed out that it is only when he believes himself to possess the express sanction of God that the pure will consent to the exercise of sex, from which otherwise he would turn in horror. For he knows that sex is a domain which belongs in a special fashion to God, and that only by the permission of the Master of life and death may he draw the curtain from its secret. From this directly follows what has also been pointed out already, that in the marriage union the pure cannot dispense with a specific reference to God. Hence, if this act is to be ennobled to the measure of perfect purity, love of the partner is insufficient, not to mention the simple purpose of propagation; an upward glance to God, thankful and loving, and abiding reverently in His sight (*in conspectu Dei*) is indispensable. The pure man perceives clearly the solemn import of the act ordained by God to give life to a new human being, and this aspect of the mystery must color everything and intensify the reference to God, providing a further motive to remain in His presence. He will never lose sight of the marvelous creative significance attaching to this act. And the quality of which this aspect is the source must further intensify the seriousness of the entire situation and the subject's attitude of reverence. But this consideration is insufficient by itself to make God in a special fashion the foundation of the entire relation. Consciousness of the divine sanction of the marriage act, given in the words "and the two shall be one flesh," the knowledge that sex is a domain specifically reserved to God, cannot be replaced by a simple reference to the possible procreation of a new human being. On the contrary, this consideration attains its full sublimity and exercises to the full its purifying power only when it springs from the background of a direct contemplation of God.

On the other hand, any proud sense of the importance of self as the author of life, that unpleasing attitude of vital passion which corresponds with a pantheist view of reality, is wholly incompatible with purity. Apart from the fact that humility is of the essence of true purity, this degradation of the wedded union to the vital plane is as such impure. Only the love which immeasurably transcends everything merely vital can ennoble this union and keep it pure. The union must be a gift of self to the beloved partner, a self-surrender which is totally incompatible with any sense of self-importance as the giver of life. The conscious reference to God must be one of humility, reverence, and gratitude, which reveals with perfect distinctness the contrast between Creator and creature, and thus completely excludes the pantheistic attitude toward God which treats with Him as on equal terms with ourselves.

It is now clear what sex is as exercised by the pure; an unconstrained, tenderly affectionate surrender of love grounded in a humble, reverent, serene, and radiant attitude. No sultry heats are here, nor grossness of triumphant flesh. Every recess is bright with the light of the soul; on everything the spirit has stamped the patent of its nobility, because every detail has become the expression of love — everything save one final remainder, whose significance as an experience, however, has, when the ideal is realized most perfectly, been rendered wholly innocuous.

We have already discovered that the perfect spirit-begotten virtue of purity is possible only as a constituent of the complete Christian character. The recognition of this is a considerable step toward understanding the connection between purity in the narrower sense and purity in the widest sense, as also between purity and the other virtues. Only the soul that *loves* Jesus, the crown of purity, can be truly *pure*. Purity also is a daughter of the queen of virtues, love. Purity, too, is one of those sublime fruits of the Holy Ghost, through whom the fullness of the Divine Love is bestowed upon us and who "brings to our mind whatsoever" Jesus "has said unto us." This truth has found a most convincing and vivid expression in Charles Gay's account (*De la vie et des verlus chrétiennes*): "We are sons of God, and as such it befits us to walk the earth with upright carriage and firm step, loins girt, eyes open, soul raised on high; to behave with sincerity, to fulfill righteousness, to live, in the words of Holy Scripture, in a fashion 'worthy of God,' giving light without, light within, light on every side, giving light by our words, by our conduct, by our deeds; to admit no thought, no love, no purpose, no act which could not endure the sight of God, nay, which does not invite it—nothing wherein He cannot take pleasure and at which He cannot rejoice. What does this mean but that every child of God must be pure in spirit, in heart and in body? How beautiful, cried the wise man, is the generation of pure souls shining with the radiance of truth. Light, purity, the God-like life, the Christian life: in God's eyes all these are one and the same."

Virginity

Introductory

"THE KINGDOM of this world and every ornament thereof have I scorned for the love of Jesus Christ, my Lord, whom I have seen, and have loved, in whom I have believed, who is my love's choice." These words which, according to tradition, St. Agnes prayed at her martyrdom and which virgins consecrated to God sing at their profession, the day of their wedding with Jesus, declare the ultimate and sublime significance of consecrated virginity as the mystery of supernatural love. Moreover, the essential nature and the incomparable magnificence of Christian virginity can be rendered intelligible by love alone, and specifically by that highest among all created loves—love of Jesus, "in whom dwells the entire fullness of the Godhead."

When in the following pages we attempt to penetrate deeper the essence and sublime beauty of consecrated virginity, and in doing so take as our starting point the consecrated maiden, we do not in any way imply that in its ultimate significance and nature consecrated virginity is different in man and in woman. There is no essential difference between the purity of a man and the purity of a woman—for the same interior attitude before God is demanded in both cases. It is the same with virginity. The essence of consecrated virginity, its specific meaning and value, which represents something entirely new as compared with purity, is the same for monk and nun; indeed, for the priest also, though in a modified form, inasmuch as the priest primarily represents Christ, not the Bride who conceives by His gift, the Church. Since, however, Scripture, to depict the nuptial relation of the soul to Christ, prefers the image of a maiden, and since it is preeminently in the office for virgins and in the rite of their profession that the liturgy speaks of consecrated virginity, the dedicated maiden will in the following dissertation serve as the typical virgin.[1] We spoke just now of Christian virginity as a mystery of supernatural love, and by so doing ascribed to it a significance analogous, though on an incomparably higher level, to that of marriage. This in turn implies that consecrated virginity possesses a wholly positive and, moreover, specifically religious value and meaning, which in no way belong to mere celibacy and which in relation to purity represent something altogether new.

---

1. In the natural order woman represents, in contrast to man, the receptive principle. This finds its clearest expression in the biological sphere, where man may be considered as the giving, fertilizing factor, woman as the recipient, though strictly speaking this is certainly true only of the external aspect of their relationship. But on the spiritual plane, even in the order of nature, woman is predominantly the receptive principle in relation to man, though here the complementary opposites are not presented so exclusively. Man is also a recipient in his relation to the world of values, and woman a giver and a creator in many departments of human life. Nevertheless, here too the receptive principle is a formal constituent of woman and belongs, as an element essential to its perfection, to the nature of "femininity," a category which cannot be confined to the biological sphere. In relation to God, however, this characteristic of predominant receptivity is not confined to the female sex. Here, where infinite and finite being, Creator and creature, God and man, meet, the man as an individual soul is as purely receptive as the woman. Here God alone is the giver, the creative and fertilizing principle, and the human being, as a creature, the recipient, therefore, if you like, "feminine." And this is preeminently true in the supernatural order of the soul as the bride of Christ the God-man. Since woman in her receptive relation to man is the obvious natural image of the soul as receptive or conceiving from and by Christ, and since we speak of the soul as the bride and Christ as the bridegroom, not vice versa, it is woman, not man, that is the natural type of that consecrated virginity, which represents precisely the nuptial status of the soul as Christ's bride. Father A. Wintersig in his fine book, *Liturgie und Frauenseele*, draws out the profound implications of the femininity of the Church. But this metaphysical femininity belongs also to mankind as a whole in relation to God. Since within the natural order the male is in the spiritual sphere, that is, in his relation to the world and human life, predominantly the creative and generative principle, he is better fitted to fulfill in the supernatural order also the giving function of the priest as the representative of Christ. Nevertheless, in this supernatural order his masculine role is confined entirely to his office—as an individual soul he must be just as receptive in relation to God as the woman, for in this order in which the Divine and the human meet, the male, inasmuch as he is a human individual, is purely receptive, that is to say, metaphysically feminine.

We must begin by making it clear that the peculiar meaning and worth of Christian virginity does not lie in its being an extension of the purity proper to the pure wife or husband, an extension which consists simply in the fact that the virgin has never had sex experience. Such a view would imply that purity and sex were somehow essentially opposed, an implication which, as we have seen, a closer analysis of the essence of purity proves to be untenable. Not the exercise of sex as such, but the manner in which it is exercised is decisive for purity or impurity.[2] Mere celibacy, the non-exercise of sex simply as such, is no advantage. The man, for example, who remains a virgin because he fails to find a wife is not, for that reason alone, in any respect purer than a pure husband. On the contrary, as compared with marriage, his state is of lower worth, not only, as is often maintained, because of its infertility, but also because it lacks the value inherent in marriage as such, as a mystery of created love. The absence of a high value cannot be in itself an advantage. There must therefore be attached to consecrated virginity some positive quality which is completely new, which invests it with such incomparable fragrance and luster and confers upon it a value not only analogous to that of a holy marriage, but far exceeding it. That is to say, consecrated virginity represents a particular form of appurtenance to God, a union with Jesus even more intimate than that possessed by every member of His mystical body, as such.

Its peculiar significance and sublime value is unintelligible from the purely natural point of view,[3] for it consists simply in this new form of union with Jesus. The consecrated virgin is always at the same time a bride, just as the virginity of the Church is also wifehood. The consecrated virgin is, like the Church, a bride of Christ, the eternal Word made flesh.[4] When we have once recognized in consecrated Christian virginity a nuptial relationship to Christ, its ineffably tender yet radiant light

2. "Beware, too, when thou art zealous for continence, that thou be not puffed up against those who are married, for they too are pure." St. Cyril of Jerusalem, *Catech.* 4.

3. "What created intelligence can grasp the nature of a virtue which is not contained within the laws of nature? Or who can find language adequate to express what exceeds the life of nature? It has come down from heaven." St. Ambrose, *De Virginibus*, I, chap. 3.

4. Cf. St. Athanasius in his Apologia ad Imp. Constantium: "Jesus Christ, the Son of God, our Lord and Redeemer, has given us in virginity a pattern of angelic holiness, wherefore the Church has always called maidens adorned with this virtue brides of Christ."

shines upon our vision, and our spirit is filled with the perfume of this mysterious state, because its positive meaning and value have been revealed to us. And it is evident without further proof that the distinctive value of virginity as a nuptial relationship to Christ, in fact, as wedlock with Him, belongs exclusively to consecrated Christian virginity, in other words, that the fact of consecration to God is a factor of decisive importance, which profoundly alters the nature of the virginity, bestows upon it its "form" (*forma*), and thus makes it the bearer of a value so wholly novel.[5]

Two questions therefore arise. First, in what does the consecration of virginity consist; secondly, what element of virginity itself enables it, if the factor of consecration to God supervenes, to become in this way a unique foundation for the most intimate union with Jesus?

5. "In virgins we do not admire the fact that they are virgins, but that they are virgins consecrated to God in holy continence." St. Augustine, *De Virginitate*, chap. 2.

The Nature of Consecration

CONSECRATED VIRGINITY IS, in the first place, freely chosen. A merely external virginity, which has not been deliberately adopted, or even is felt as an unwelcome and painful trial, has as little to do with consecrated virginity as outward poverty forcibly imposed has to do with poverty freely chosen. No doubt, a person who is a virgin against his or her will can also be pure, but that purity has, as we have already pointed out, no advantage whatsoever over wedded purity, for it brings with it no new value.

On the contrary, the attitude of such a person to sex continues the same as that of a virgin, male or female, before marriage, until all intention of marriage is finally renounced. But this renunciation does not in itself imply a positive choice of virginity, that is, a determination to belong to God in a special fashion. Even when the circumstances of her life have brought a woman to the conclusion that she is called by God to celibacy and this conviction leads her to renounce matrimony, this is not necessarily an explicit choice of virginity in the positive sense. The renunciation, indeed, alters her attitude to sex as compared with that of a virgin before marriage, inasmuch as it signifies its interior exclusion. It is, however, not a solemn profession of virginity, but a simple acceptance of it, as a man might accept poverty he had not freely chosen, but which God had imposed upon Him. Even though—as would be the case if the renunciation were felt as painful—the resignation to God's will possesses a special value, that value in no way differs from that involved in every submissive acceptance of a cross which God lays upon us. In such a case, therefore, no new and distinctive value attaches to the fact of virginity as compared with wedded purity; there is simply the value which submission to God's will, here as in all other circumstances, brings with it. The same value, for example, is present when an unhappy marriage is borne submissively as the dispensation of God's Providence.

Or, again, we may consider a different case. Virginity is here regarded by the subject as her normal condition, because she has no thought of marriage. In this case, no doubt, the virginity is in a certain sense deliberately chosen, as it was not in the previous instance; but with consecrated virginity it has nothing whatever to do. There can be no question of a special value attaching to such virginity. Whether it is deliberately adopted or practiced as the obvious course—in any case it is not chosen for the sake of its sublimity and profound significance. It is simply the effect of a purely natural inclination, and as such represents an absence of value as compared with marriage. It is the mere consequence of a defect, inasmuch as the subject is, at least so far as she is personally concerned, incapable of the high value which marriage represents. No greater good occupies her heart in its place: there is nothing but a personal insusceptibility. No doubt such a person may be pure, in which case all the loveliness of purity which we have depicted ennobles her being, but the purity is based, not upon the virginity, but on a general attitude which can equally exist in the married. It is therefore evident that the mere fact of physical virginity as such confers no sort of advantage over marriage, but rather involves a certain lack of value.

But even when virginity is freely chosen for the sake of some noble object it is still divided by an entire world from consecrated virginity. If, for example, a woman renounces marriage in order to remain with her parents or chooses a profession whose external conditions exclude marriage, as that of a school teacher in many countries—virginity is indeed freely chosen, but since its distinctive and profound religious significance is not among the factors which determine the choice, it does not necessarily effect a close relation to God. Nor is it even sufficient that virginity be freely chosen because for one reason or another it is believed to be the will of God that the subject should remain in that state, as a man might be convinced that it was God's will that he should adopt some particular secular profession. If, for example, I become convinced that my parents' illness and need of help is a message from God, bidding me renounce marriage, that does not make my virginity in any way consecrated to Him.

The virginity must be directly chosen for God's sake, and for no other reason; and, moreover, in order thereby to belong to Him in a special fashion. It is not sufficient that it be chosen as *willed by God*; it must be referred to Him far more directly; it must be actually *consecrated to God*. It is so consecrated when, in accordance with the words of Our Lord and Savior Jesus Christ, it is freely chosen "for the kingdom of heaven's sake" (*propter regnum caelorum*). Jesus said to his disciples: "All cannot receive this saying, but they alone to whom it is given. For there are eunuchs which were so born from their mother's womb; and there are eunuchs which were made eunuchs by men; and there are eunuchs which made themselves eunuchs for the kingdom of heaven's sake. Whosoever is able to receive it, let him receive it" (Matt 19:11–12). The words which state the motive for which consecrated virginity is to be chosen, *propter regnum caelorum*, have been differently explained. They are frequently understood of the heavenly reward which awaits the continent. But on this interpretation that which confers upon virginity a peculiar character and a unique value is simply passed over. And, which is the most weighty consideration, this interpretation leaves the specially close relationship to Jesus which this virginity constitutes wholly unexplained. Nor yet, if the words are to be taken as a statement of the motive for which consecrated virginity is chosen, am I able to accept Fr. Wintersig's interpretation, that by *regnum caelorum* we are to understand the Church. Our Lord's words are clearly intended to state, not the objective *raison d'etre* of virginity, the reason why there should be virgins, but the *motive* for which the state of virginity should be chosen. The expression "kingdom of heaven" possesses so general and inclusive a meaning in the Gospels, in which "for the kingdom of heaven's sake" so often means the same as "for God's sake" or "for His glory," that it may also be understood as a general statement of the only motive which suits the context. We may again recall the words ascribed to St. Agnes: "The kingdom of this world and every ornament thereof have I scorned for the love of Jesus Christ my Lord, whom I have seen and have loved, in whom I have believed, who is my love's choice." Only when virginity is chosen for the love of Jesus, to belong to Him in a particular and closer fashion, and thus to give a special glory to God, does it possess the character which makes it consecrated virginity. Only the will of the individual, who out of love will give herself more closely to Christ, is able—so far as the motive is concerned—to transmute a merely physical into a consecrated virginity. A purely external consecration to God made by the Church over the head of the individual—a contradiction in terms, since it is incompatible with the nature of the Church— could never constitute consecrated Christian virginity.

This can be seen most clearly by comparing with the Christian virgin the consecrated heathen virgin, the Vestal. Not only does the virginity of the Vestal lack the lifelong obligation, whereas Christian virginity, as we shall see later, must of its very nature be *perpetual*, but, what is most important, the virgin's free choice is wanting. The Vestal virgins were selected and appointed without their consent being asked. And this of itself excludes the motive for which Christian virginity is freely chosen, the love of God, which alone can bring it into a real relation with Him. The heathen virgin was treated as a mere thing and handed over to the god or goddess as a piece of property.[1] This fact altered the entire complexion of this pseudo-religious virginity.[2] Virginity is here regarded from

---

1. Cf. also the description of ritual purity above: chap. 6, sec. c.

2. An opponent may possibly bring forward the Vestal virgins and the priests of Pallas. What sort of a chastity is it which is based, not upon the free practice of virtue, but only on the purely exterior circumstance of age, which demands no perpetual renunciation, but on the conclusion of a specified time is required no longer." St. Ambrose, *De Virginibus*, Bk I, chap. 4.

a purely natural standpoint and represents something purely vital. It does not transcend the domain of physical sex. Whereas Christian virginity with its supernatural radiance destroys every hankering after the charm of sex, with this natural virginity this is by no means the case. On the contrary it is, so to speak, from the sexual point of view that this virginity is valued. We need only contemplate the impassable gulf which divides the natural vital ideal of virginity as exemplified in Artemis from the hallowed chastity of the most blessed and ever Virgin Mary.

The most radical distinction, however, between heathen and Christian virginity, that which determines this absolute difference of quality between them, does not consist simply in the fact that the former lacks the free choice indispensable for a genuine self-dedication to God and the love which is its motive, but primarily in this: the deity to whom the pagan virgin was consecrated was a false god, not the true God, One in Three, who reveals Himself to us in Jesus. Moreover, heathen virginity does not owe its form to the operation of the supernatural union of human nature with God effected by the Incarnation of the eternal Word and the consequent nuptial relationship of the Church and Jesus. But it remains true that the *kind* of consecration also determines the difference of quality between the two. The love of God, here the indispensable motive, which is essentially grounded in God's infinite love for man, whom He so loved that He gave His only begotten Son, and which is actually a participation of this Divine Love, is thinkable only within the mystical body of Christ.

Consecrated virginity, therefore, can exist only when a member of Christ's mystical body freely chooses perpetual virginity, out of love for Him, and, moreover, in order by that virginity to belong more closely to Him. But even this is not enough. Yet another factor is essential — the explicit vow of virginity. It is by the social act[3] of vowing that the vir-

---

3. The vow obviously represents something entirely new, over and above the determination of the will. In a work which deserves to be called a classic. *Das Apriori im burgerlichen Recht* (Ges. Schriften, Halle, 1921), Adolf Reinach distinguishes a special type of acts which he calls by the general name of "social acts." The imparting of information, the promise, the question, the command, the request, the expression of thanks, and so on, constitute this group of acts distinguished by the common feature that they cannot be really performed unless another party takes cognizance of them.

gin first places her virginity in the hands of God and solemnly binds herself to it.

The distinctive nature of consecrated virginity as compared with every other is now clear. Only when the virginity is freely chosen out of love for Jesus in order to belong more closely to Him and to give glory to God, and, moreover, vowed in perpetuity, does it become consecrated virginity.[4]

But the question now arises, why it is precisely *virginity* which, when consecrated to God, establishes a bridal relationship to Jesus? I can solemnly vow other things out of love to Christ — poverty, for example, or fasting or other forms of mortification — and although such vows do no doubt unite me closer to God, they do not establish a specific bridal relationship essentially transcending the bridal relationship which belongs to *every* member of Christ's mystical body. There must be a special and mysterious reason for the fact that it is virginity alone which, when consecrated to God, produces this unique union with Jesus.

They are acts of whose essence it is to be recognized. They necessarily include an external expression, cannot in fact be fully performed mentally, for example, like acts of love, admiration, and determination. To this group belong also those creative acts whose performance creates specific external obligations; for example, the obligation toward another which results from a promise, the contractual relationship arising from a contract, or the obligation established by the command of a lawful authority. The vow also belongs to this special type of social act. As contrasted with the mere will to do some particular thing or even the mere announcement of that intention, which create no external obligations, the vow, which is closely related to the promise, constitutes such an external bond. In the case of virginity it is the vow which alone can effect that outward bond, just as it is the matrimonial vow and ceremonial act as opposed to the mere will to belong to another in love which constitute the external tie of wedlock.

It is impossible here to investigate in detail the distinctive nature of these creative social acts. I must refer my readers to Reinach's work. But a word must be said as to the distinctive material quality of the vow as compared with the promise, oath, and so on. In the first place, the vow necessarily involves a direct reference to God, which is not the case with the promise. Though a promise may so to speak be given *in conspectu Dei*, that does not essentially alter its nature as such. The reference to God is most direct when He is invoked as witness to an oath. But such an oath in another respect differs typically from the vow. The subject of a vow is essentially restricted to the future conduct of the vower. I can only vow that I will behave in such and such a fashion. But I can also swear that I have done or omitted something in the past. Indeed, my oath need not relate to any personal conduct of mine, its subject may be some objective fact.

4. So St. Thomas: "Virginity as a virtue requires the determination sealed by vow to remain a virgin perpetually." *Sum. Theol.* II-II, q. 152, a. 11, ad 4.

CHAPTER TEN

The Nuptial Relationship with Christ Common to All Souls in Grace, and the Special Marriage of the Consecrated Virgin

VIRGINITY MUST possess a particular quality which, when made fruitful by the special intention involved in consecration to God, establishes a bridal relationship to Jesus of a wholly novel kind. The very language in which Jesus speaks of virginity points to the mysterious depths which it conceals: "He that is able to receive it, let him receive it."[1] The passages in which He commends poverty lack this mysterious hint. It enables us to answer the second of the two questions we formulated at the outset and determine that quality of virginity which enables it to constitute a bond with Jesus of so special a character. And at the same time it presents us with the key to the particular objective value and significance of consecrated virginity.

---

1. The words "he that can receive it, let him receive it" are usually so understood that "receive" (χωρεῖν — *capere*) is explained, not as "understand," but as "embrace." Let him who is called to virginity, accept it — that is to say the man in whom the ground has been prepared for this vocation, as contrasted with the man who may indeed understand and grasp the significance of virginity, but for whom its beauty involves no personal call. Whichever interpretation be correct, in any case the language here used of consecrated virginity is peculiarly solemn and mysterious. On any interpretation the characteristic contrast remains with other passages which speak of poverty.

Like the Church herself, every member of Christ's mystical body is a bride of Jesus. Jesus is the bridegroom of every soul which is a member of His mystical body. Why, then, is the soul of the consecrated virgin in an entirely new sense His bride?

To this question also different answers have been returned. According to some, the more strictly a person represents a constituent part of the Church, the more fully is the nuptial relationship between Christ and the Church realized in him. The priest, the religious, the nun, the deaconess of the primitive Church, are constituents of the Church in a stricter sense than the other members of Christ's mystical body. Therefore the nuptial relationship to Jesus is more strictly realized in them. Since these vocations involve virginity (or celibacy at the least), virgins are brides of Christ in a stricter sense than are other Christians. But this answer only removes the problem a step further. For if the virgin is wedded to Christ only because she belongs in a closer degree to the Church, our question must be repeated in another form. Why does virginity possess this significance for those members of Christ's mystical body who are in the stricter sense representative of the Church?

To this question the following answer will perhaps be given. The reason why this significance attaches to virginity is because the Church herself is a virgin. Only those persons can completely display in themselves the holy life of the Church who resemble her in this central point. It is on account of the resemblance and conformity with the virgin Church, Christ's true Bride, that virginity possesses such a decisive significance for the relation of the individual to Christ. But this answer also merely shifts the problem. It raises the further question. Why is the Church a virgin, and what does her virginal character signify? And it has told us nothing about the nature of the fundamental profound and intrinsic connection between virginity and wedlock with Christ. That was simply taken for granted when the Church was denominated a virgin. However, we must try to discover it in the virginity of the individual, since in this literal virginity the factors here in question, which are also to be found in the Church, are present in a far more accessible and visible form and, from our human standpoint, at first hand. For although the virginity of the

Church is no mere poetical metaphor, but a reality in the fullest sense, nevertheless for our understanding the point of insertion into the natural order, that is to say the type which belongs by its visible aspect to nature, is the obvious point of departure. We must therefore have already distinguished more closely the characters of virginity and the relations between them in this more accessible sphere before we can decide whether the proposition implied by the answer just put forward is true—namely, that to create the nuptial relationship with Christ in the more distinctive sense the consecrated virginity of the individual does not suffice by itself, but that the virginity of the Church is, strictly speaking, its foundation.

When we ask which element in virginity establishes the new and distinctive bond with Christ the usual answer is: The virgin is undivided—*indivisus est*. This answer appeals to the well-known passage of St. Paul: "He that is unmarried is careful for the things of the Lord, how he may please the Lord; but he that is married is careful for the things of the world, how he may please his wife, and is divided. She that is unmarried is careful for the things of the Lord, that she may be holy both in body and in spirit; but she that is married is careful for the things of the world, how she may please her husband" (1 Cor. 7:32–34). This undividedness may be understood of many elements in virginity, and is therefore capable of different interpretations. Hence the further question arises: Why and in what respect is the virgin undivided in her surrender to God? The explanation given in the passage just quoted is predominantly psychological: "He that is unmarried is careful for the things of the Lord, how he may please the Lord." The division in the aim of a man's life which normally results from marriage is presented as a division of his surrender to God. But St. Paul's words do not justify us in concluding that for him this explanation is intended to state the fundamental nature of the undividedness which virginity secures, that for him this psychological effect of celibacy is the ultimate and entire significance of the virgin's freedom from division. In any case, a closer examination of the nature of virginity reveals further and more profound reasons for the undividedness, which are, we must conclude, also embraced within the Apostle's scope.

We must now attempt to discover all those features to which virginity owes its significance as a special and a closer union with God, proceeding gradually from the more obvious aspects to the more profound. And we shall, of course, devote particular attention to the "undividedness," which we shall examine at length, with the object of discovering the various factors which produce and represent it.

Baptism makes us partakers in the Divine Life of the most Holy Trinity, inasmuch as it is the means whereby we are admitted into Christ's mystical body. In Christ divine and human nature are joined in a union which infinitely exceeds anything to which the name of marriage could be applied. Such a union of both natures in one Person is unique, found only in the God-man Himself. But every baptized person by his membership of Christ's mystical body shares in this union with the Divine Nature, though in an incomparably less direct fashion. The manner in which the Trinity inhabits the Christian soul by sanctifying grace can be appropriately expressed by comparing it with marriage. But the relation in which Christ stands to every baptized soul, although its mystery obviously transcends all our concepts, can be symbolized with far greater adequacy by this the highest of all human relationships. The relationship between Christ and the soul is therefore termed a marriage.[2] But leaving out of account this mysterious objective relationship, which may exist even when there is nothing to reveal its presence, for example, in the baptized infant, we will inquire into the special relationship of the individual soul to Jesus and its attitude toward Him, as experienced by that soul. From this point of view the relationship to Christ possessed by the majority even of the living members of His body is far less intimate than anything to which the term "marriage" could be fittingly applied.

What is the essence of the nuptial relation as opposed to other bonds of love?[3] Among all the forms of human love wedded love is the deepest, closest, and most splendid. I am not speaking here of marriage, but of the

---

2. "Whatever the position of a man in other respects, whatever the relationships which bind him to the earth, from the moment his soul is in the grace of God, it is the bride of Christ." Charles Gay, *De la vie et des vertus chrétiennes*, Vol. II, x, de la Chasteté.

3. We are not concerned here with that specifically tender quality, so full of promise, which distinguishes the love of the engaged as opposed to the love of the wedded, but of that fundamental category of love represented alike by the love of the engaged and the wedded as contrasted with other categories, for example, love of parents or love of children.

love between the married or the engaged. The distinctive quality of that love consists first and foremost in the specific *correlation* of both lovers; in the fact that in this case, to a far higher degree than in the love of parents, children, or friends, the person *as such* is the exclusive "matter" of the relationship. And this, of course, is bound up closely with the fact that this is a love in which both partners complete each other in a unique fashion, possible only between the two sexes.[4] For this completion the distinction between male and female, as a difference of the entire personal type, is of primary importance, and it can be effected even where the very thought of physical union is wanting. In nuptial love—to put our point in another way—both parties *live*, as it were, *for each other*, not side by side. It is the noblest of human relationships and the most effective in arousing both partners from the dull callousness which has become man's second nature; the relationship in which both parties, as it were, stand face to face, looking into each other's eyes. Each exists for the other. For this love is uniquely directed toward union with the beloved. A friend's love desires contact with that friend in order to embrace some third object in a common gaze; parents' love is eager to share in the child's life; but the bride longs to be *united* with her lover, to share in his *being*, an aim which presupposes a distinctive mutual adaptation and the possibility of a fundamental mutual completion.[5] The mysterious glory which invests nuptial love and its perfection as the crown of human relationships has nowhere been depicted so vividly as in the Song of Songs: "Come, I said, let me arise and go about the city. In the streets and in the open spaces I will seek him whom my soul loveth: I sought him, but I found him not. The watchmen that go about the city found me. [To whom I said] Him whom my soul loveth have ye seen? Hardly had I gone from them, when I found him whom my soul loveth. I laid hold on him and would not let him go, until

4. We must, however, be very careful not to understand this unique mutual completion in a pantheistic sense, as though man and woman did not by themselves constitute a complete nature and the perfect human being was only brought into existence by their union—a view to be met with in German idealism and in romantic literature. Nor is nuptial love fundamentally a selfish desire for completion, but a response to value of which a desire for union is the consequence. The quality of completion is but a secondary feature of this love.

5. See further my observations upon the *intentio unitiva*, which is indeed an element in every love, but attains its fullest development in nuptial love.

I had brought him into my mother's house, and into the chamber of her that bare me. I adjure you, O ye daughters of Jerusalem, by the gazelles and by the harts of the field, that ye stir not up, nor awaken love till it please.... Set me as a seal upon thine heart, as a seal upon thine arm: for love is strong as death; jealousy is cruel as the grave: the flashes thereof are flashes of fire, its flames are the flame of lightning. Many waters cannot quench love, neither can the rivers drown it: if a man should proffer all the substance of his house for love, he would be utterly despised" (Song of Songs 3: 2–5; 8: 6–7).

The essential elements of wedded love we have already seen must be present also in our love for Jesus. Abbot Columba Marmion in his *Sponsa Verbi* (The Bride of the Word) depicts in noble and expressive language the different degrees of relationship to Jesus:

"We have heard Jesus Christ Himself on more than one occasion compare the kingdom of God to a wedding feast. God in and by His word invites souls to the banquet of divine union.

"At a banquet several classes of people are present. First the servants. Respectful to the master of the house, they stand upright and carry out the orders given. In return the master pays them the wages on which they have agreed. If they perform their duties well he thinks highly of them. But he does not admit them to his table or to his friendship, nor does he tell them his secrets. They are the type of those Christians whose conduct is habitually inspired by servile fear. Such persons treat God as a Master, a great Lord, whom, like the servants of the Gospel, they occasionally find too 'hard'; they only do that to which they are strictly obliged, and from fear of punishment. These souls, who still live in a spirit of bondage, in fear are excluded from personal relations with God.

"Then there are the guests, the friends. The King has invited them to His table, has spoken to them in language which supposes mutual goodwill, shares with them his food and wine. But there are different degrees of this friendship. They are the type of Christians who love God without having given Him *everything*. When they are with the King He shows them His favors, but they are not always in His company. They leave Him for their own business, and show their friendship only at intervals.

"When the friends have left, the *children* remain. They belong to the house; are at home and stay there. Bearing their father's name, they are the heirs of his possessions; their life is devoted to knowing their father, obeying and loving him, and in return he entrusts them with confidences from which the friends are excluded. They represent those faithful souls who live and behave as God's children, who realize perfectly St. Paul's description: 'Ye are no more strangers or sojourners, but ye are fellow citizens with the saints and members of the household of God' whose delight it is to practice the virtues which distinguish a child of God—faith, hope, and love—virtues whose perfect exercise is a total abandonment for their heavenly Father's good pleasure. 'Whosoever are led by the Spirit of God, these are sons of God.' To these child souls God communicates Himself as the sovereign Good in which all their desires find fulfillment. Finally there is the *Bride*. From her the Bridegroom has no secrets; she shares with Him the closest intimacy in the tenderest love; no union is more perfect than hers. The union between husband and wife far surpasses that between parents and children. 'A man,' our Lord tells us, 'should forsake father and mother and cleave to his wife.' No union exceeds this for intimacy, tenderness, and fruitfulness."

This supreme and most intimate bond between the soul and Jesus, this nuptial love and union with the Incarnate Word, is, as such, confined to no special vocation. Every baptized person can attain it with the help of grace, for this kind of love and union with Christ is the mark of the saint. And as there can be saints in every walk of life, and kings may be saints as well as hermits, married women as well as virgins, laymen as well as priests, so there is no station or vocation which can exclude a soul from this supreme relation to Jesus, because the ultimate vocation of every man is not the exercise of the profession in which he happens to be, but the most perfect conscious realization of that sublime union with Christ, objectively created by baptism.[6] A bride's love for Christ and her supremely close intimacy with Him belonged as much to St. Elizabeth

---

6. "Every creature spiritualised, elevated and deified by faith becomes Christ's sister; and when that faith blossoms into love the sister becomes the bride: 'my sister, my bride' are the words in the Song of Songs. No doubt there are degrees within this relationship —innumerable degrees, possibly as many as the souls that love. 'The bride,' says St. Bernard, 'is every soul that loves.' Even those who have thought fit to bestow on a human being the hallowed name of bridegroom have not on that account lost the right to call their Redeemer by that name." Charles Gay, op. cit. II, x.

or St. Catherine of Genoa[7] as to St. Catherine of Siena or St. Teresa, to St. Louis as much as to St. Francis. Nevertheless, there is a state of life that may be termed the state of perfection and which stands in a special relation to wedlock with Christ. It is, we may say, a form of life that is the external expression of this marriage which is its special aim. It is the life of poverty, chastity, and obedience chosen for Jesus's sake, or life in accordance with the evangelical counsels.

We shall now examine in detail to the best of our ability the relationship between this state of perfection and the interior marriage with Christ, and what are the grounds of the special correspondence between this form of life and the soul's nuptials with Him. We shall thus acquaint ourselves with the various respects in which virginity and wedlock with Christ are united, and finally catch a glimpse of that profound and mysterious aspect of virginity in virtue of which consecrated virginity, and it alone, constitutes an objective marriage with Jesus.

---

7. One day a Dominican Friar, "perhaps to test her [St. Catherine of Genoa] or because of some mistaken notion, told her that he himself was better fitted for loving than she, because he having entered Religion and renounced all things both within and without, and she being married to the world, as he was to Religion, he found himself more free to love God, and more acted upon by Him. And the Friar went on and alleged many other reasons. But when he had spoken much and long, an ardent flame of pure love seized upon Catherine, and she sprang to her feet with such fervour as to appear beside herself and said: 'If I thought that your habit had the power of gaining me one single additional spark of love, I should without fail take it from you by force, if I were not allowed to have it otherwise. That you should merit more than myself is a matter that I concede and do not seek; I leave it in your hands; but that I cannot love Him as much as you is a thing that you will never by any means be able to make me understand.' And she said this with such force and fervour, that all her hair came undone, and falling down, was scattered upon her shoulders. And yet all the while her vehement bearing was full of grace and dignity. And when back at home and alone with her Lord, she exclaimed: 'O Love, who shall impede me from loving Thee? Though I were not only in the world as I am, but in a camp of soldiers, I could not be impeded from loving Thee.'" (*Vita della. Caterina Fiesca Adorna*, quoted and trans. by Baron F. von Hugel, *The Mystical Element of Religion*, vol. I, pp. 140-41.)

CHAPTER ELEVEN

The Ascetical Significance of Virginity

As a result of the Fall there remains in man, even after his redemption, a downward trend, a tendency to pride and concupiscence. Even when his conduct is on the whole governed by the determination not to offend God, this downward impulse does not cease to exist, and his behavior all too easily displays a certain alloy of these vices. I am not thinking of those attitudes of concupiscence or pride which are grievously sinful, because they involve a deliberate rebellion against God, and which are therefore present when a man falls into mortal sin, nor yet of venial sin, but of man's general weakness toward himself, his disorder, and the attitudes in which this imperfection is expressed. What joy is there in successful work, in the service and goodwill of others, in the very performance of duty, even in graces received, which is unmingled with a drop of self-satisfaction, pride, and selfish pleasure? What delight in the possession of a beautiful house, in the prestige of an exalted position, is wholly devoid of greedy self-love? What enjoyment of even lawful earthly goods pleasant to the senses, well-cooked food, for example, rare wines, or a soft bed, is altogether free from gluttonous indulgence, sloth, or passive yielding to desire? The life of the average Christian who avoids mortal sin and seeks to avoid venial sins, so far as he recognizes them—but who with no qualms of conscience surrenders to the obvious tendency of nature by concessions to self-love, and never shakes off this comfortable indolence, never emerges from the pleasant, warm stream of life—is still penetrated by pride and concupiscence, though they have certainly been expelled from the center of his being, and have lost the sovereignty of his person.

The imperfection of such a Christian, the remains of pride and concupiscence with which his life is still permeated and alloyed, oppose an insuperable barrier to complete union with Jesus. Such Christians may be servants of the Lord, possibly even His friends, but never children, not to mention brides. Purification, therefore, from these relics of the spirit of the world, which still cleave to the soul, these remains of "the lust of the eyes, the lust of the flesh and the pride of life" has always been regarded as an indispensable prerequisite for that full and ultimate union which distinguishes the bride of Christ. To accomplish this purification is the task of asceticism. Asceticism calls upon us to renounce the enjoyment of lawful goods, even if in itself it involves no indulgence of the pride and concupiscence which still cling to us, because the renunciation closes and keeps closed the outlet for certain fundamental instincts and strengthens the dominion over pride and concupiscence of a self which humbly and reverently loves.

That asceticism of this kind demands renunciation even when there is no actual danger of lapse into pride and concupiscence is further shown by the fact that it not only prohibits or limits the enjoyment of certain goods, but also requires the deliberate choice of certain evils. The discipline and the spiked belt, for example, to mention only two instances, are more than a renunciation of goods, they are a voluntary choice of evils. They may indeed be employed purely as a sacrifice[1] or as temporary aids to overcome temptation.[2] But their normal use is as a means of mortifi-

---

1. Penance as a sacrifice offered to God lies, of course, entirely outside the sphere of asceticism.

2. For example, when St. Benedict and St. Francis plunged into thorns in order to destroy by the physical pain the fascination of the temptations which assailed them.

cation; that is to say, to prepare the way by a special training for the necessary supremacy of the humble, reverent, and loving self over concupiscence and pride. This choice of evils is obviously not intended to repress in a concrete instance the operation of these vices, but to interrupt normal comfort and physical well-being, in itself harmless, in order to free the spiritual person generally from its weakness toward the body and its instincts.

Sleep, for example, is in itself a divinely ordained refreshment of the body. Asceticism, however, requires not simply the restriction of sleep to the amount which reason shows to be necessary, that is to say, a refusal to make any concession to sloth, but in addition vigils, the mortification of a hard bed, and so on. By denying himself things which, like the normal measure of sleep, are in themselves no yielding to concupiscence, but which, nevertheless, necessarily involve a contact with the domain in which concupiscence operates and which provides an outlet for the body's elementary need of refreshment, man should gradually so free himself from bondage to that domain that even his unavoidable contacts with it, as in sleep, eating, drinking, and so on, no longer involve any danger of surrendering to the remains of concupiscence. That is to say, the thoroughly legitimate use of certain good things is renounced for the purification thus effected. This refusal to open the natural outlets for certain elementary needs—for example, the urge to sleep, eat, drink, speak—is a mortification, a means whereby the spiritual person is set free from the life of the instincts and acquires a mastery over the entire domain of concupiscence.

Asceticism, however, has another purpose. It requires the avoidance of every situation which involves the danger of entertaining emotions of pride or sensuality. Dainty dishes, for example, are refused because *in a particular instance* one is afraid of giving way to gluttony; a soft bed renounced for fear of yielding in any way to sloth; wealth, lest an undue delight in possessions should take hold of their owner; outward honor and success, lest they prove an occasion to gratify the stirrings of pride. In such cases the renunciation is not a method of self-training in order to make essential progress, a means of purification, but a prudent and wary avoidance of every occasion which might involve the danger, not primarily of mortal sin, but of the deliberate indulgence of an imperfection and ultimately of venial sin.

Both points of view may be termed ascetic, though the significance of asceticism is more typically expressed by the former. Detachment from earthly goods for an ascetic motive is, therefore, essentially distinguished by the negative character of the object against which the struggle is made, namely pride and concupiscence. What, then, is the relationship between asceticism and virginity? We cannot answer the question until we have investigated more thoroughly the specific intention which determines the ascetic attitude toward certain goods. As we have already pointed out, even the entirely legitimate and innocent enjoyment of many good things provides, in the first place, a certain outlet for man's elementary instincts, secondly an opportunity for the indulgence of the relics of concupiscence and pride in fallen human nature, and thus involves in itself a certain danger of excess. To curb these instincts, even when the opening of the outlet would not lead to any excess, an explicit renunciation of pride and concupiscence is necessary, which, when inspired by the right intention, is at least a disciplinary method by which we free ourselves from their yoke. Delight, for example, in owning a fine house, or in beautiful dresses, is certainly not wrong in itself, but can very easily involve, even quite unconsciously, the indulgence of what St. John calls the lust of the eyes, a characteristic mixture of pride and sensuality.

In any case, the free choice of a life of purity and the renunciation of all possessions provide a direct method by which the lust of the eyes can be completely overcome, whereas the innocent enjoyment of property, even when it does not lead to any deliberate excess, is, at any rate, no such instrument of purification. External freedom, the ability to do or leave undone what we will—of course only within the limits of what God has not forbidden—that exterior independence for which youth longs so passionately, is no doubt something genuinely good which it is perfectly legitimate to enjoy, but it may easily prove the indulgence of a disordered desire of freedom and a certain pride. This is the pride of life mentioned by St. John. In this case also the voluntary renunciation of this good is a direct means of self-emancipation, which the ordinary freedom, though in itself innocent, obviously is not. Similarly that high and holy good, marriage, involves, if even as a completely unintended by-product, contact with the sphere of fleshly lust, and with it the inevitable danger of yielding to its unconscious gratification. But for this very reason to refuse relief to the sting of the flesh is a peculiarly efficacious method of mortifying the flesh, which married life, even when the exercise of sex is confined to its highest function, cannot afford, since the act of wedded union always involves, however little it be deliberately sought, an outlet for the demands of sex.

The evangelical counsels—poverty, obedience, and chastity[3]—prescribe the external road to holiness, in which heroism renounces even those goods whose use is by no means sinful, indeed in itself good. Their purpose is in the first instance ascetic. As complete continence, consecrated virginity constitutes a union with God, in so far as it represents at the same time the entire renunciation of fleshly lust. The purpose of asceticism, here of primary importance, is purification by self-denial, since purification is a *prerequisite* for the perfect union with God. Its other purpose, the radical avoidance of all occasions involving the danger of a slip, may also play a part. But from this ascetic standpoint *the virginity as such* does not constitute a closer bond with God; on the contrary, that bond must be sought only in the heroic determination born of an extraordinary love of God to renounce any and every good rather than incur the risk of being separated from Him by some lapse.

That is to say, considered from the ascetical standpoint, virginity lays the foundation of the closer union with God, but from this point of view the union with God which virginity as vowed continence creates is not specifically *nuptial*. It may indeed subserve the nuptial relation, inasmuch as it is an *effective means* to effect that union with God which wedlock with Jesus, in the sense of the allegory worked out above, involves. But

---

3. The term "chastity" must be here taken in the sense of complete continence, not in the stricter sense explained above.

in this respect it represents nothing essentially new as compared with poverty and obedience. They, too, are methods of purification of decisive importance. That is to say, the ascetic standpoint cannot provide the answer to our question; it cannot represent the factor in virginity which makes it and it alone the ground of a unique marriage with Christ.

CHAPTER TWELVE

Virginity as Undividedness

THE ASCETIC, however, is not the most profound or most distinctive meaning of the evangelical counsels.[1] As we penetrate the significance of this state of life we become aware of a further element of great importance: undivided appurtenance to God. If a man is bound to earthly goods his heart also must be still occupied with them and cannot be given wholly and undividedly to the things of God. This truth is expressed in the parable of the great supper. "A certain man made a great supper; and he invited many: and he sent forth his slave at supper time to say to them that were invited. Come, for all things are now ready. And they all with one consent began to make excuse. The first said unto him, I have bought a field, and I must needs go out and see it: I pray thee hold me excused.

---

1. That the value of virginity is not confined to its ascetic aspect is also the sense of St. Ambrose's sublime panegyric: "'The scent of thy garments,' saith the bridegroom, 'is more delicious than the scent of all spices,' and again, 'the scent of thy garments is like to the odour of frankincense.' Lo, what a progress is here! Thy former scent exceeds, saith he, the spices which surrounded the Body of our Saviour in the tomb; it sheweth that the disordered motions of thy body have been slain, the lust of the flesh dead. But thy latter scent is likened to the odour of frankincense, it is exhaled from the purity of our Lord's Body, from the blossom of virginal chastity."

And another said, I have bought five yoke of oxen and I go to prove them: I pray thee hold me excused. And another said, I have married a wife, and therefore I cannot come" (Luke 14:16–21). The freer the heart from earthly ties, the more unreservedly can it belong to God. We are not now concerned, as when we were discussing the ascetic aspect, with the struggle against something in itself worthless, against the relics of pride and concupiscence, but with a renunciation of earthly goods of a lofty and noble nature, in order to exclude the danger of perverting the relation which should obtain between Creator and creature, by attaching the heart to a created good more closely than is consistent with the divinely willed order, and so dividing it between God and creatures.

The motive is no longer purification, but undividedness in the strictest sense—the inner emptiness indispensable if we are to be filled with God, complete inner freedom. From the ascetic standpoint renunciation becomes less necessary, the higher and nobler the good; the danger of excess being correspondingly less, the less can its renunciation be regarded as a mere penance, the less appropriate is it as a simple disciplinary method. It is no accident that the object of asceticism as a specific discipline is chiefly the superficial goods, that this asceticism consists mainly in fasting, vigils, scourging, mortification of the pleasure of the eyes, and so on, and not primarily in renouncing the enjoyment of great works of art or noble friendships. But the danger of dividing the heart, on the contrary, is from one point of view greater, the higher and nobler the good in question. We must, however, remember that every good thing of high rank, when rightly understood and used, also, as we shall see later, unites the soul with God; moreover, the nobler it is, the more effectively does it fulfill this function.

Virginity produces an undividedness in its subject, as being not simply the complete renunciation of *fleshly lust*, but the renunciation of that *community of love and life* which marriage represents. This renunciation of the highest earthly good is for that very reason preeminently the way to achieve undividedness, for man's heart is here in the greatest danger of being divided. The division which marriage may produce can assume many forms. As a result of its community of life and love the heart may easily become absorbed too deeply in the beloved, the gaze be no longer directed exclusively to God. "He that is married careth...how he may please his wife." Thoughts, wishes, interests easily become divided; that is, they will not be referred to the other party only *in* God and according to the due scale of values: regard for the partner's interest in the first place will be isolated as an end complete in itself, and, secondly, will violate the true order of values and so thrust itself between God and the soul. This danger may reveal itself by a superficial distraction of the thoughts and attention from God. In consequence of man's restricted field of attention, which holds good also in the emotional sphere, married people are particularly exposed to the risk that their thoughts, wishes, and interests—in short, the actual content of consciousness—will be so exclusively occupied by the beloved and the myriad concerns of their common life in the world, that they do not live for God, but at best are content to avoid breaking His commandments. Moreover, the married man has his duties as such; as a married man he lives in a special sense *in* the "world"; he is obliged to attend to many worldly matters, which the married state—still more the foundation of a family—involves. If he permits all his thoughts and interests to be absorbed by these things, he becomes a servant of God, a friend at best—he cannot be a child, still less a bride.

But the most profound threat to single-minded service of God does not come from the distraction or dispersal of a man's powers which marriage tends to effect by the bond with the world that it sets up. It consists rather in a division of the fundamental aim of life, which the mutual love and common life of wedlock directly tend to produce. Since our very nature makes it difficult for us to keep our hearts in and for God, if noble earthly goods entice us and take strong hold of our affections our hearts all too easily depart from the order which should be observed between God and the creature we love. The danger is not, indeed, that we should love a creature too much, for the love of one creature for another is greatest when that love is a participation of Jesus's love for the beloved, that is to say, a love *in* Jesus. It is the danger of a disordered love which, without being any greater for that—it is, on the contrary, necessarily less, love of a less perfect kind—sets itself up as its own sufficient end, in isolation from God, and therefore absorbs the lover and withdraws his heart from Him. Even if the will still belongs entirely to God, the heart is no longer completely His. That man may be God's servant, friend, even child—but not His bride. For the bride's heart belongs to Jesus, the God-man. This element of danger implicit in every created love is increased immeasurably by marriage, because marriage in its unique, intimate, indissoluble and lifelong partnership constitutes objectively "a life for another" as does no other partnership between creatures.

But if virginity as a state of singleness avoids this division, is undivided in the double sense just explained, nevertheless from this standpoint also it enjoys no essential advantage over poverty and obedience. The danger of division is also incurred by the man who owns wealth, or who devotes himself to the profession or avocation of his choice. Attachment to money or possessions can also involve division in two ways, still more devoting one's life to a profession. Moreover, the higher the rank of a secular profession the greater the danger. How easy it is for art, science, or politics to absorb the strength and thoughts of a great artist, scientist, or politician, to capture his heart and thus divide it, so that he may indeed be God's servant or friend, possibly even His child, but His bride never—that is, when the work is not done in and for God, but dominates the worker as an end in itself.

Virginity therefore as the state of undivided application to God has at most a superiority of degree over poverty and obedience, inasmuch as marriage, as the highest earthly good, involves the most profound danger of division, a danger, moreover, for which compensation is made by the fact that, as we shall shortly see, marriage as the highest earthly good from another point of view also unites the soul closest with God.[2] But the point on which we must now insist is that undividedness in the sense just discussed cannot provide the key which unlocks the mysterious significance of virginity as the foundation of a unique relation to Christ. For since poverty and obedience—if perhaps in a lesser degree—are also indispensable conditions of undividedness, from this point of view virginity does not differ from poverty and obedience in such a way as to explain how the virgin in virtue of her virginity is wedded to Christ in a peculiar and mysterious sense.

2. We should remember that marriage is a sacrament—therefore not only something holy but also a means of grace, and in this fundamental and most strict sense a bond of union with God.

CHAPTER THIRTEEN

The Positive Mission of Natural Goods and the Condition under Which Their Renunciation is Supernaturally Fruitful

BEFORE PROCEEDING with our analysis of the state of perfection, which we undertook in order to isolate the element in virginity on which the special connection between virginity and wedlock with Christ is based, we must touch briefly upon the positive function served by the possession of genuine natural goods, in order to complete what we have already said of the dangers to a life in and for God which the possession of these goods involves. Although this consideration of the positive function of that which consecrated virginity renounces may seem at first sight a digression from our theme, it is in reality indispensable if we would understand its secret as wedlock with Christ.

We forget at our peril that every superior good has a specific mission to perform toward the soul, a distinctive aid to afford it on its way to God the "Father of Lights." We do not refer to that positive ethico-religious function which belongs also to the lower goods in so far as they are genuinely good: inasmuch, that is to say, as the use of inferior goods provides man with a legitimate outlet for the primary instincts of his nature, it preserves him, as we have already seen, from the separation from God which their unlawful and inordinate indulgence would involve; and from this point of view every good of this kind can exercise explicitly a religious function, if it is used by someone who has learned to regard good things in general as expressions of God's loving kindness, benefactions of the Father Who makes His sun shine upon the just and the unjust.

This aspect, however, is not in question here. On the contrary, we are concerned with the specific mission to our soul, wholly different from the former, which is peculiar to the goods of *superior rank*, those goods which as sources of happiness are contrasted with those goods which provide only pleasure or satisfy bodily needs. Every good of this category—for instance, life in a beautiful, noble, and cultivated environment, a liberal profession which is a source of happiness in itself and intrinsically of high value, freedom from external obstacles to the development of a man's intellectual powers and talents, opportunity to steep oneself in the sublime beauty of nature or art or to enjoy the intimacy of some noble character—any one of these goods represents a gift of distinctive quality to its possessor. Contact with the values objectively present in such goods —for example, the beauty of a work of art—definitely raises above it the soul that perceives and appreciates their worth, and brings it nearer to God. The instant a high value really takes hold of the soul it awakes to its proper state. Returning to itself, it is brought back from the circumference to the center, becomes recollected and is lifted, if but for a moment, above the indolence and dullness of its normal condition. As Plato put it, its "wings grow." That self which loves in humility and reverence, to which values make appeal, becomes for the moment at least absolute master of pride and concupiscence, which, surely, dissolve within the man who has been genuinely moved to tears by some object of sublime beauty. Does he not at such a moment break through the shell which has hardened over his soul—pierce the dreary mist that covers it like a pall? Is not that soul at such a time better disposed for everything that is good? And when some high value has really taken hold of us does it not seem to us as though scales had fallen from our eyes, as though now for the first time we beheld the genuine countenance of reality, the world of things as they truly are, which hitherto had always escaped the vision of our weak eyes, darkened by the fog of everyday life? And do we not feel as though the dividing barriers of human respect and selfish isolation from our fellows had dissolved like spray, as though we remembered that, in the profoundest depth of our being, we are immediately united with all men, because we are, as it were, in the presence of God? And the higher the value, the more surely does it produce effects of this kind.

Contact with high values leads us, therefore, to God; in the first place, inasmuch as it brings into action within us the self that humbly and reverently loves; secondly, because the value in question utters its *sursum corda* to the heart of man, and draws his gaze upward to God. But we are now concerned, not with the case in which values simply take hold of us, but, more than this, with the *possession* of the corresponding goods. Does possession of a superior good as such, that is, *qua* possession, lead our souls to God? It does—and also for two reasons. In the first place the close contact with the good in question, which its possession implies, involves a further contact with the values it realizes, whereby they produce the effect just described in a new and more intense fashion. Thus, for example, the man who hears the performance of some masterpiece of music is in far closer contact with the world of loveliness it contains than he who merely thinks of that work as something known to him. The former is exposed in an entirely different way to the rays of its beauty. Similarly—though in a somewhat modified sense—the man who has been permitted the intimacy of a noble character basks in the light and heat of his worth to an extent which essentially exceeds that to which they are enjoyed by the man who simply perceives and honors that worth from a distance, without the opportunity of closer contact. Thus the possession of a good at least makes it easier for the values it contains to take hold of its possessor and produce their intrinsic effect upon the soul. Indeed, in many cases possession alone makes the production of this effect possible, though this breaking-through is always an extraordinary state, which mere possession of the good in question can never permanently guarantee.

The specific function which the possession of the higher goods fulfills as such becomes still clearer when we consider it from the following point of view. In every man who is not wholly sunk in apathy there lives an urge after happiness and satisfaction of some kind or another. The possession of some good thing of high rank and noble quality emancipates a man from attachment to inferior goods, inasmuch as it opens to him, as we have just seen, a region of his soul far deeper and far more his own, and satisfaction at this deeper level enables him to dispense with the gratification of more superficial desires. It is a very usual experience. The part played in our lives by eating, drinking, sleep, and surface pleasures and comforts of every kind, becomes far less if our soul is powerfully and deeply moved by some higher good; for example, by meeting a dear friend after long absence. We feel ourselves freed from the petty craving for the shallow gratifications of everyday life. We can no longer even understand how some deprivation of comfort could be a matter of serious annoyance, when our heart is filled by a profound joy, for example, the recovery of someone we love from a severe illness. Contact with a good of this kind always supplies us with an intrinsic standard by which to measure the lower goods. When we are in possession of the superior good, attachment to the inferior seems ridiculous and outgrown.

Moreover, the attachment to a good and the desire to possess it is the more unselfish, in proportion to the depth and nobility of that good, in other words to its degree of value. Devotion to the goods which produce happiness, such as art, or deep-rooted ties with others, is essentially less egoistic than devotion to goods which give pleasure, such as palatable dishes, good wine, bodily comfort, and so on. For as contrasted with the latter, the former is necessarily founded upon a genuine response to value. The man who cannot rejoice at the existence of beauty in art or nature or of noble characters, who cares nothing for such values in themselves, can receive no happiness from the possession of that to which they are attached. From this standpoint also it is easy to see that the possession of the higher goods, when they are fully understood and appreciated, brings us nearer to God. For to outgrow attachment to the inferior goods which give pleasure is to become deeper, relatively to overcome egoism, and to penetrate further into the world of values.

Lastly, it is in its possession as such that the good in question is recognized as a gift, and the soul thus lifted in solemn thankfulness out of its everyday routine. When, that is to say, the values attached to goods take a profound hold of us, the possession of such goods is experienced as a special effect of God's goodness toward us; we feel ourselves surrounded by His loving providence, are forced to our knees and our glance drawn upward to Him in heartfelt gratitude — "for His mercy endureth forever." And this element of heartfelt thanksgiving is also a powerful solvent of pride and concupiscence and introduces us, as it were, directly into the presence of God. The mission of the higher goods of this world to bring us nearer and yet nearer to God, inasmuch as in proportion to their rank they free us from pride and concupiscence and lift the soul above its lamentable attachment to lower goods, is seen most clearly in the case of the highest earthly good — namely, marriage; principally, of course, Christian marriage. Over and above the profound efficacy of every real love between human beings — whether it be the love of parents, children, brothers and sisters, or friends — in freeing and uplifting the soul and leading it to God, the complete community of love and life peculiar to marriage possesses, when understood and experienced in the right way, a specific power to shatter pride. Profound love for the partner with whom life is henceforward to be spent in common frees the soul from attachment to superficial goods such as property, power, external honor, worldly success. Who does not know that when perfect communion with another soul fills the heart to the brim with unspeakable happiness, to renounce all other good things is an easy matter?

Yet not wedded *love* only, but the *self-surrender* of marriage also, is distinguished by its power to emancipate, to cleanse the heart of pride and concupiscence. The unreserved surrender of the spouses, the union of two human beings in mutual love — sealed for life by God's sanction solemnly imparted, and secured by its objective validity against the caprices and vagaries of fallen man — the plighted obligation of fidelity till death, signify an entrance into the profoundest natural depth of the soul. Moreover, the specific fulfillment of mutual wedded love, the craving to become completely one, which the union of wedlock involves, has from this standpoint an extremely important function to fulfill. We have already seen, when we were treating of purity, the profound significance of the marriage act as emancipating the very center of the personality. Because it represents a unique self-surrender, it destroys, when experienced and accomplished in its highest form, a stiff self-containedness which tends to harden the heart, blunt the susceptibilities and produce a self-important prig.

This forsaking of self, this deep and noble happiness of wedlock which draws the glance upward to God in heartfelt gratitude, frees a man alike from proud self-adherence and from petty attachment to comfort, to the pleasures of the table, and to frivolous amusement. The man who has been vouchsafed the supreme earthly happiness of a perfect marriage and who, with unremitting appreciation values the gift at its full worth, must become increasingly emancipated from those other earthly goods of inferior value. What sacrifice of earthly goods would a St. Elizabeth or a St. Jane Frances de Chantal have deemed too high a price for the happiness of their marriage in the hour when they were faced with the loss of their husbands?

This is not the place to study in full the sublimity of marriage and show in detail how this supreme fellowship of love and life between human beings leads us to God. We must be satisfied with the indication just given.[1]

We now come to an important point. If a genuine earthly good is renounced for the religious motives already mentioned, that renunciation can possess the value there ascribed to it only if the mission normally fulfilled by the good in question of freeing us from inferior goods is really *transferred*—that is to say, if the void left in the soul by the absence of that good is filled by God and the realm of supernatural values. It is the nature of fallen man to seek compensation for every cross which God lays upon him in something which gives pleasure—usually in some lower pleasure. We need only reflect how seldom a great and deep sorrow—the loss, for example, of someone dear to us—is really endured and experienced to the full, how seldom the soul abides in her

---

1. I refer the reader to my book *Marriage* (New York: Longmans, Green, 1931). Consult further J. Mausbach's important writings on this subject —also on points discussed earlier.

depth, and lifts her gaze to the sovereign Good that her sorrow may be transfigured by a glory from above, her void filled, and with Him whom sin alone can lose. How readily, after a great sorrow, we abandon ourselves to a listless apathy,[2] how readily seek compensation for ourselves in shallow gratifications, among which may be work for its own sake; how often we attempt by distractions or routine, or by a lazy drifting on the stream of superficial experiences, to shirk the cross which God has sent us.

If to receive a cross laid upon us by God in the right way, to understand His divine purpose in sending it, to allow it to bring us nearer to Him and to avoid all compensations of a lower order, presents our religion with a task of no small magnitude, the problem is doubled whenever any earthly good is freely renounced. Our responsibility now is obviously of a wholly different kind, since it is *our free choice* which has renounced this particular good. However heroic and noble it may be at the moment, the renunciation can be finally acceptable to God only if He and love for Him fill the void that has been left and compensations of a lower kind do not creep in unnoticed. This is preeminently true of virginity. The danger of compensation from below is greater here than in the renunciation of any other earthly good. We saw above the peculiar mission to free the center of the soul which belongs to the supreme earthly partnership of love and life, its uncompromising summons to conquer pride and concupiscence and the natural aids it brings to that conquest. The dangers which the absence of so valuable a good may involve are obvious. How easy it is for the man who has renounced the delicious, gently liberating happiness of the highest earthly partnership to fall into pettinesses and attachment to lower goods; above all, how easily may the heart become hardened, and love, because that person remains in a very literal sense unemancipated, turn wholly to bitterness. That particularly close appurtenance to God, as bride of Christ in the sense of our allegory, which consecrated virginity is intended to create,

---

2. Of course, by "apathy" we do not here mean the psychological exhaustion which, as a purely nervous reaction, follows a severe blow.

can only be effected if there is no attempt at compensation from below.[3] The soul must by this renunciation really secure in another way everything which in marriage specifically unites her with God. Every other earthly good, especially all attachment to inferior goods, such as the desire for honor or power, natural delight in success, curiosity, the craving for excitement, exaggerated sensibility, not to mention such purely negative things as envy, malicious pleasure in the hurt of others, cruelty, and so on, must give place, and one thing alone occupy the soul: the supernatural love of Jesus, "in whose heart dwells the entire fullness of the Godhead."[4]

Who, then, will presume to make free choice of permanent virginity and forever renounce so lofty a good as marriage, if virginity fulfills its purpose and possesses its value, if it signifies a close appurtenance to God, only when the void it creates is not compensated from below? Who dare claim that he can dispense with the power of married love to free the heart and raise it above the rest of the world? He alone who invokes and invites Jesus, "the desire of the everlasting hills."[5] God's call to the soul is a thing wholly supernatural, with which no message indirectly transmitted by other goods can be compared. "Follow me," Jesus spoke to Matthew, and "he arose and followed Him." That call leaves no room for further question. He who invites the soul to the state of perfection will fill

---

3. We may here recall what St. Ambrose demands from a consecrated virgin: "The virgin's purity consists in the integrity of her entire nature. The words that come from her lips, free from all bitterness, and full of sweetness and charm, are her virginal children" (*De Virginibus*, Bk. I, chap. 8). And again: "Thou must know thoroughly Him whom thou lovest—the entire secret of His being" (ibid., chap. 9). Tauler also: "In festo sanctorum omnium: The bride of Christ therefore must always be so minded that in nothing does she wish to please any one save God, if she will truly be called and be His bride."

4. Obviously the natural effect of the renunciation depends to a very large extent upon the intention with which consecrated virginity is chosen. But the most decisive factor will only become clear to us when we have learned what it is that constitutes the distinctive secret of that virginity.

5. St. Anselm touches indirectly upon the decisive part played by vocation in the choice of virginity when he writes: "But every man hath his own gift from God, one thus, that is to say, that he should live in complete continence, but another thus, that wedded to one wife he should have connection with no other woman. The text is sufficient proof that not only continence is God's gift, but also the chastity of the wedded. Since, therefore, both have been shown to be God's gifts, we know from whom to ask them, if we have them not, and to whom our thanks are due, if we have them" (*On 1 Cor. 7*).

her with Himself if she obeys His invitation. The religious or nun, however, is not therefore dispensed from the necessity of keeping special watch, lest resentment in one form or another intrude, or compensation be sought in some inferior good for the higher goods which have been sacrificed. On the contrary, religious must be constantly on their guard: on the one hand never to console themselves for what has been abandoned by some lower indulgence, on the other to keep themselves effectively at a distance from the good which they have heroically renounced. But that which without God's call would be presumption, with it becomes an act of heroism. For the call justifies them in expecting that the renunciation of natural aid will be supplied by supernatural aid. To such St. Ambrose's words are applicable: "But you, holy virgins, enjoy a special protection, because in your inviolate virginity you keep troth to your Lord. And indeed it is no cause for wonder, if the angels fight for you" (*De Virginibus*, Bk. I, chap. 9).

It is therefore essential to consecrated virginity that it should be an answer to the call of Jesus. Not only must it be freely chosen out of love for God with the intention of belonging more closely to Him; it must also be the answer to the mysterious invitation that Jesus addresses to the soul.[6] It is this call which makes it something altogether supernatural. This truth finds expression in the sublime Preface for the profession of nuns. "Look down, O Lord, on these thy handmaidens who place the profession of their continence in Thy hands and bring to Thee the oblation whose purpose Thyself hast inspired. For how should the spirit enmeshed in mortal flesh overcome the law of nature, the craving of sense to take its freedom, the power of custom, and the sting of youth, if Thou,

---

6. Wherein this call of Jesus consists is another question. A miraculous intervention, as in the case of St. Paul, is obviously not required. The well-grounded conviction that we have been "called" may be reached in all sorts of ways. But an enthusiastic admiration of the religious life is never sufficient. The individual conviction that one is "called" is not, however, the important consideration. Greater weight must be attached on the one hand to Jesus's general call embodied in His commendation of this state of life to everyone "who can receive it"; on the other to the external confirmation of the subjective belief by the spiritual director, and by the head of the order when a novice is admitted to profession. It is precisely by this external confirmation that the objective reality of a vocation, as opposed to a merely subjective enthusiasm, is expressed and guaranteed.

O God, didst not in Thy clemency enflame their free wills with this love of virginity, if in Thy loving kindness Thou didst not nourish this desire in their hearts, and if Thou didst not bestow the needful strength for its achievement?"

It is now clear that virginity, as that renunciation of marriage whose motive is religion in the sense explained above, involves at the same time the renunciation of a great help on the way to God and therefore requires a special intention which transforms the renunciation into a transference of this function of marriage; it must be accompanied by special care to avoid all compensation from below, and before all else must be rooted in the conviction of an objective call from Jesus. We must keep all these factors well in mind when we now return to our problem, what it is that makes consecrated virginity in a peculiar sense a marriage with Christ.

CHAPTER FOURTEEN

Virginity as an External Form of Life and the Outward Sign That All Things Are Forsaken for Jesus's Sake

WE HAVE ALREADY seen that, from the standpoint of asceticism and undividedness alike, the state of perfection represents a special way of belonging to God and constitutes a closer bond with Christ than other forms of the Christian life. We must point out, in the first place, that this is equally true from quite another point of view. We have considered hitherto how the religious life produces in practice a closer bond with God, is a path to that ultimate union with Him, enjoyed by the bride of our allegory, a means of purification and a guarantee against division. But it is also in itself an external expression of the life that is specifically for God. To stand before God naked, the world renounced for Jesus's sake, to abandon the life of the world in order, as it were, to dwell in the presence of God (*in conspectu Dei*), to die to the world and self and live only with the life of Jesus, is distinctive of the religious state as a form of life, even quite apart from its psychological results for the individual. Just as marriage as a state of life is the external expression of unity between two human beings, apart from the union between the spouses which is a psychological effect of marriage as this unique community of life, "religion" as a form of life expresses life *for* God, unreserved appurtenance to Him. For in it the truth that "one thing is necessary" has assumed a concrete shape, its very existence is a witness to this word of eternal life. It embodies in visible form a preference of God to all His creatures. It therefore possesses in itself an objective value and significance, in itself it glorifies God, quite apart from the ascetic progress and the avoidance of division which may be its consequences. Normally, no doubt, these consequences ensue, and in turn by their psychological operation effect a closer union with God. But it obviously possesses this significance and value only when consecrated to God in the sense already explained, in other words, when it is truly an embodiment of love for Him.

But apart from the fact that life in poverty, obedience, and chastity bears the external stamp of life for God, and is the adequate external expression of that interior attitude toward Him which distinguishes the mystical bride, this point of view discloses a new and characteristic motive for which the religious life is chosen. "Religion" is not only a way to closer union with God, it is also its result. Not only does the state of perfection as a form of life reflect outwardly the attitude of a bride; the choice of it is also an actual consequence, an organic embodiment of this fundamental union with Jesus. Love impels us to express the self-surrender it involves, to give it an external shape. It takes delight in sacrifice for the beloved, desires to show him that he is loved before and beyond everything else. The earthly bride leaves her parents' house, breaks away from her life with those whose love has hitherto been her environment and to whom she belonged, in order to follow the man whom her love has chosen. Likewise the soul that is inebriated with the love of Jesus desires to forsake everything for His love, to stand before Him naked, listen for His voice alone, draw His glance into her heart, and with loins girt and lamp burning await the Bridegroom. Thus to forsake all things, to renounce the most precious treasures which in this life God's goodness bestows upon us, to surrender every possession to Him, "the fairest of the sons of men," to break away, the moment His call is heard, though surrounded by the most pressing obligations and bound by the closest ties, and to let go everything which was, so to speak, within our grasp, that henceforward our gaze may be fixed unswervingly upon Him and our arms outstretched in His worship—this constitutes a specific embodiment of this unmeasured and adoring love.

It is impossible in this connection to consider the many points of view from which the excess of her love for Jesus drives the soul along this heroic road of total renunciation. Not only does "religion" perpetuate, as it were, the soul's reply to Jesus's call to forsake all things for His sake, a reply which constitutes a peculiar organic expression and embodiment of love; it also appeals to the soul's love for the Crucified, as a way of the Cross, a way of suffering and self-denial. The soul chooses suffering, to be conformed to Him who took upon Himself the suffering of the world, and to carry the Cross with Him; she will suffer that she may bathe in Jesus's wounds and in her suffering be wedded to Him in a unique way; she will suffer because to suffer is to die, and to die for Christ, to lay down life for His sake, is the supreme expression of love and life in Him. The entire secret of the supernatural love in which the life of the saint consists, expressed in St. Paul's words: "For me to live is Christ and to die is gain," here dawns upon our vision.

Even without attempting to distinguish the different factors (their strength continuously increased by their combination) which impel love to choose a life of poverty, obedience, and chastity, it is plain that we have to do here with an entirely new standpoint, wholly distinct from the ascetic or from that of undividedness, which enables us to understand why the state of perfection denotes a close form of appurtenance to God, or, in other words, is the appropriate external embodiment of man's highest love for Jesus. Not only does the love which finds its expression in the forsaking of all things for Jesus's sake, its fulfillment in the choice of suffering and a life of sacrifice for Him, represent, simply as such, a special bond with God inasmuch as it is the principle of the bride's life, the solemn act in which that love issues; the choice of a life in poverty, chastity, and obedience signifies the conclusion of a bond with God, closer than that possessed by every living member of Christ's mystical body. This deed of love constitutes a close form of appurtenance to God. Not every deed motived by a supreme love of God creates as such a bond of this kind. The mere fact that it is inspired by such a love is not enough. If, for example, a man from love of this kind vowed to fast for the rest of his life on bread and water, his vow would not in the same way produce a state of close union with God. The radical abandonment of the world, the standing before God naked, the renunciation of the highest earthly goods, the choice of the Cross, the death, which are effected by poverty, obedience, and chastity and by these alone, constitute not simply one among many possible results of a supreme love of Jesus, which could express itself equally well in some other vow, but the intrinsic and organic expression of that love, its objective embodiment. This, of course, does not mean that this supreme love and the intimacy with Jesus it involves is confined to those who choose the state of perfection. St. Elizabeth, St. Catherine of Genoa, St. Frances of Rome, St. Louis, and a host of other names bear witness that the soul's inner relation to God is independent of her external state of life. But it remains true that the state of perfection as such, as a visible organic embodiment of this sovereign love, is the form in which a special appurtenance to God finds expression.

The three different points of view from which the state of perfection constitutes a close form of possession by God, asceticism, undividedness, and the forsaking of all things for love, are obviously not disconnected. On the contrary, they are united by a close intrinsic bond, and, moreover, the higher point of view includes in a certain sense the lower. He who is truly undivided must already have been purified, or, at any rate, must will to be so, and he whose love is such that he will forsake all things because Jesus calls, and will follow Him on His way of the Cross, is already undivided and purified, or at least, has the will to be so. Ideally, indeed, when the world is renounced to live for Jesus alone in poverty, obedience, and chastity, one single act of supreme love of Jesus and of self-surrender to Him unites all these factors in an organic whole.

It is therefore not only as a means of purification and of attaining undividedness that virginity constitutes a special form of possession by God, but also inasmuch as the state of consecrated virginity is the external embodiment of the choice to forsake all things for Jesus's sake. The renunciation of marriage as the highest earthly good embodies that choice in an even more expressive form than the renunciation of property or freedom to be one's own master.

"Lo, we have forsaken all and followed Thee; what then shall we have? And Jesus said unto them, Truly I say unto you, that ye who have followed me, in the regeneration when the Son of Man shall sit on the throne of His glory, also shall sit upon twelve thrones, judging the twelve tribes of Israel. And everyone that hath left houses, or brethren, or sisters, or father or mother, or children, or lands, for my Name's sake, shall receive an hundredfold and shall inherit eternal life." Is this possibly the clue to the secret which makes the virgin the bride of Christ in a sense so much stricter than is applicable to any other soul, and which invests virginity with so exquisite and heavenly a fragrance? Does it, perhaps, consist in the fact that the choice of virginity is the distinctive deed of that love which forsakes all for Jesus's sake, inasmuch as the renunciation of the partnership of life and love constituted by marriage is the greatest and most profound renunciation, and because the dearest, the noblest, and the greatest thing in the whole world is given up? Is this the secret of which Our Lord said, "Who can receive it, let him receive it"? It is not. The man who leaves his wife for Jesus's sake makes the same choice with the same irrevocable determination. But in this latter case the element of integrity, a specific factor of the special bond with God, is wanting. No doubt, virginity is a typical case of forsaking all things, but it is not the only one. The decision to forsake everything on the spot, to wrench oneself from the dearest ties at the call of Jesus, is also typically accomplished by those who, like several apostles, leave their wives.

But the most conclusive proof that the clue is not to be found here is the fact that, so far as this function is concerned, virginity does not differ essentially from poverty and obedience. Like these, virginity represents, though in an even higher degree, the forsaking of all things, and thereby effects as they do, if in a greater measure, that close union with God which from this standpoint expresses in a particularly characteristic form the attitude of the bride in our allegory; but in this respect it involves no completely new element as compared with poverty and obedience. We must therefore look for yet another factor, a factor peculiar to virginity alone, which will explain why the consecrated virgin is the bride of Christ in a far more literal sense than the person who is wedded to Christ only in the sense of our parable.

CHAPTER FIFTEEN

The Secret of Virginity as Wedlock with Christ

To DETECT that unique and mysterious factor of virginity on which the wedding with Christ is based we must recall that natural mystery we discovered in sex. We saw that in a certain sense sex is the secret of every human being and that the disclosure of this secret to another creature and the delivery of it to that other in wedlock constitutes a self-surrender and self-donation of a wholly unique kind. Even the supreme and most complete surrender of the soul to some other human being who is dearer than life itself and in whose soul we plunge our own by a profound mutual discovery and understanding in Jesus, is, nevertheless, not equivalent to that mysterious external self-delivery which takes place in the act of marriage. This may seem a hard saying, since the surrender of the heart to another is something higher and more valuable than the surrender of the body. But just because the surrender inherent in love as such is in itself something higher and nobler, its content is far more inexhaustible; it is, indeed, in the last resort a participation in the infinite love of Jesus. Unlike the latter it belongs to eternity; not only surviving beyond the grave, but only then attaining its most perfect fulfillment and a completeness which corresponds to its lofty rank as a quality. While still confined by the limitations of his earthly life man is unable to surrender himself in love of this kind so decisively, so entirely, so objectively, and so irrevocably. On earth it is not in our power without the cooperation of the body to give our heart to another creature in the same way as when the body plays its part. In eternity alone will it be possible. The sacrifice of one's life denotes a somewhat similar surrender, inasmuch as in that sacrifice already here on earth a human being surrenders himself as this numerical individual, this complete whole. There can be no doubt that many saints who were not martyrs, St. Francis, for example, have possessed a love far greater than is necessary for a man to shed his blood for God. But the martyr's death is, notwithstanding, a unique gift of the entire self.[1] Similarly, the self-surrender of sexual union, in which we lay bare to another the secret of our own person and share in that of another person, finds no analogy among any other relationships between creatures. By the sexual union and by it alone can that donation of self be made in which the entire man is given as a complete unit, and which constitutes between the partners a nuptial bond, a union of a wholly unique kind.[2]

The act which places this sexual secret in the hands of Jesus inviolate and sealed forever denotes a self-surrender to Him and marriage with Him which corresponds with the matrimonial self-surrender to a creature.[3] Since Jesus is a heavenly bridegroom, marriage with Him must be completely different from earthly wedlock, a purely spiritual union. Nev-

---

1. The existence of a mysterious analogy between martyrdom and virginity has been felt from the beginning. See St. Cyprian, *De Habitu Virginum*, Chap. 2; or *Venantius Fortunatus, De Laude Virginum*, Lib. 8. "Amidst the ranks of apostles and holy prophets the virgin receives the highest rewards after the martyrs." (*Inter Apostolicas acies, sacrosque Prophetas; proximo. Martyribus praemia Virgo tenet.*)

2. It is from this standpoint alone that the strict exclusiveness of the bond created by the partnership of marriage can be understood. Here also lies the explanation of the fact that this exclusiveness, arising out of the nature of wedlock as such, ceases with the death of either partner, whereas the bond of love and the merely relative exclusivity based upon it, in other words, fidelity to the beloved, is in no way affected by death.

3. "From the time thou didst dedicate thyself to perpetual virginity thine own has been no longer thine own." St. Jerome, Ep. 8. *Ad Demetriadem.*

ertheless, there is a fundamental feature really common to both. That supreme self-surrender of the entire person—analogous to the surrender of life for another—which can be given to a fellow creature by marriage alone, is here made to Jesus by the vow never to disclose this secret to anyone, by the radical and final renunciation for His love of all exercise of sex, and by cutting oneself off from the world to live for Him alone. Only those who have grasped the utterly central position occupied by sex, its depth, and the mystery that invests it, of which we have attempted an investigation earlier in this book, are in a position to grasp the mysterious factor which makes consecrated virginity wedlock with Christ, and explains its unique sublimity, its soft and heavenly radiance, its bittersweet perfume. The final renunciation of the exercise of sex made by the consecrated virgin shifts her psychological center of gravity in an altogether unparalleled fashion. By that renunciation she dies to the world and partakes of something that otherwise would be possible only in eternity. A center within herself is in a sense set "free," which she discloses to Christ alone and whose surrender to a fellow creature is indissolubly bound up with the disclosure of sex. The zone of our personality which constitutes, so to speak, the point of insertion in our nature for Jesus's love and whence in turn proceed the acts which He accepts, in other words the place where He knits up a fellowship with us and entertains with us a mysterious converse, is different from the psychological plane of contact with creatures.[4] By the solemn and final renunciation for Jesus's sake of that unique gift of self to a creature in which marriage consists, by the determination to keep one's secret perpetually hidden, indeed, to surrender that secret inviolate into the hands of Jesus, sex is in a sense abolished and the center of gravity in that person raised to the level specifically in contact with Him. In

---

4. If the act of marriage when accomplished in the highest way destroys a certain stiff self-containedness which tends to harden the heart, blunt the susceptibilities, and produce a self-important prig, this peculiar self-containedness is destroyed by marriage with Christ in a far more complete and radical fashion, since in this case also the secret of the self is surrendered, but the distinctive escape from self is accomplished in an entirely different, and at the same time far more profound, manner. That is to say, whereas in marriage the release is, as it were, the natural counterpart of the self-imprisonment, wedlock with Christ lifts the person altogether above the sphere of sex and thereby effects on a higher plane everything and more than everything which the mere release effected on the lower.

this case and in this case alone is a radical transcendence of sex effected. Take the case of a girl who, for love of a man whom for some reason or other she is unable to wed, solemnly promises *for his sake* to remain a virgin for life. Because of her love for him she will never give herself to another. A promise of this kind constitutes, no doubt, a close bond with the beloved, and, above all, prevents the separation which marriage with another would involve. But she is not thereby married to the man, and still less does she, in the fashion just mentioned, leave sex as such behind her.[5] Altogether unlike the virgin who simply accepts with resignation the non-exercise of sex or whose virginity belongs to any of those other types we have discussed and is not consecrated to God, the person of the consecrated virgin really transcends sex, and that most profound and intimate region that in all other human beings is inextricably bound up with sex is, as it were, absorbed in the purely spiritual zone which is the field fertilized by the dew of Jesus's love. By this act of surrender the consecrated virgin gives her secret to Jesus and marries him in a fashion really analogous to earthly wedlock, though her marriage is purely spiritual and involves no sort of *qualitative realization* of sex. At the same time that peculiar spiritualization is effected which stamps her entire life as a victory over the world and invests it with a fragrance redolent of eternity.[6] Even here on earth the bride of Christ lives, not only a *pure* life, but a life like that of heaven, where "they neither marry nor are given in marriage." Though the physical fact of sex does not cease to exist, nor are temptations to impurity excluded, Christ's bride, in virtue of her wedlock with Him, objectively transcends sex, and beyond and above it her soul shines clear and bright before God. "'A garden enclosed art thou, my sister, my

---

5. The heathen virgin, the Vestal, represents in its grossest form the mere transference as opposed to the transcendence of sex. Her renunciation of sex simply transfers its possessor from a human being to a divinity anthropomorphically conceived, in the same way as it might be preserved for a man. Her state of life, therefore, does not in any way involve a transcendence of sex. It must now be perfectly clear why this heathen virginity is to be regarded as wholly sexual in its conception.

6. That consecrated virginity contains a mystery far exceeding the mortification of the flesh and, so to speak, descending upon the virgin from above, when she accomplishes this unique surrender of herself to Christ, is beautifully expressed by the words of Pope Liberius which St. Ambrose quotes in his *De Virginibus* (Bk. III, chap. 1): "In thee who hast long been a foe to the corruptible pleasures of the natural man, He (Christ) will implant the sublime secret of virginity."

bride; a garden enclosed, a fountain sealed.' Such is the praise which Christ pronounces on those who have attained the goal of virginity, and He sums all up in the single word 'bride.' For the bride must be espoused to her Bridegroom and bear His name; she must abide spotless and inviolate, like a sealed garden, wherein every scent of heavenly perfume is shed abroad, where Christ alone may enter and gather what grows therein of incorporeal seed. For the love of the Word is not for the body, seeing that His nature is not such that it can take hold of corruptible hands, feet, or countenance. Only incorporeal and spiritual beauty attracts His desire, and in it alone does He take pleasure; the body's beauty touches Him not."[7]

We must now have at least an inkling of the reason why consecrated virginity, and it alone, constitutes a marriage with Christ, totally different from the bond created by poverty and obedience. The vow here is not simply the solemn promise of something to God, but a *betrothal* (*desponsatio*) in which the vower is herself the subject of her vow—in fact, a genuine marriage. It is possible to be a bride of Christ in the interior subjective sense of our allegory without being wedded to Christ in this objective fashion, just as we can feel wedded love toward a fellow creature without being actually married to that person. Marriage is the specific external embodiment of this love, inasmuch as it completes the supreme interior communion of hearts by an exterior and formal union, and creates an objective indissoluble bond whose worth and validity are guaranteed against caprice and which is as such independent of love's ebb and flow. In like manner the vow of the consecrated virgin is the organic expression of her love and the means by which the interior bond is projected into the external sphere; it creates, in fact, a new tie between the virgin and God, objective, irrevocable, and of a peculiar intimacy.[8] "No creature can surrender itself more completely to God than the virgin who thus weds her Lord. For, like the holy city in Scripture whose 'founda-

---

7. Methodius of Olympus, *Banquet of the Ten Virgins, or Chastity*, quoted by Fr. Athanasius Wintersig, op. cit.

8. Our analogy must certainly not be pressed too literally, since in relation to God every interior state or event is always a fuller and more objective reality than it is in relation to creatures.

tions are upon the holy hill' this union, knit as it is by a vow for eternity, has its birth outside the realm of mortal things, and is not exposed to their hazards, not even to the possibility of regret. Not one of the many states of union with God is comparable with the hallowed contact that, in the presence and under the protection of that powerful witness, the Church, weds to Jesus Christ the soul that dedicates herself to chastity. In so exceptional a degree do such souls become His brides that in the ordinary language of Christians the title is specially attributed, if not altogether reserved, to them. It is theirs to understand in full measure what to others is spoken only in parables; theirs to enter the King's palace; theirs, and theirs alone, to 'follow the Lamb whithersoever He goeth' and sing to Him the anthem whose music is known only to themselves."[9]

Moreover, the mystery which the sacrament of marriage signifies — the nuptials between Christ and His Church — is expressed even more directly by consecrated virginity, since the virgin and the Church are wedded to the same husband, Christ.[10] Nowhere else do we find the secret of consecrated virginity as the mystery of supernatural love, a nuptial relationship to Christ and a marriage with Him, stated in language at once so sublime and so expressive as throughout the entire office for the profession of nuns. "Thou hast in every generation poured forth Thy graces upon all peoples under heaven and hast made them, in multitude like unto the unnumbered stars, the heirs of Thy new covenant; but among all the presents which Thou hast bestowed upon Thine own — who are born not of blood nor of the will of the flesh, but of Thy Holy Spirit — certain souls have received from the wellspring of Thy fullness a special gift. Without detracting by Thy ban from the honour of wedlock, and Thy nuptial blessing resting still upon the holy state of matrimony. Thou yet hast willed that chosen souls of loftier purpose should reject the bodily intercourse of men and women, but attain the secret that it comprehends; who do not copy what marriage does, but devote their entire love

9. Charles Gay, loc. cit.

10. On the other hand, from another point of view the consecrated virgin remains betrothed so long as her earthly life lasts, the final union being reserved for eternity, that union of which marriage between creatures is but a type. We are, however, fully justified in calling virginity a marriage with Christ, since the self-surrender presents a close analogy with physical wedlock.

to the mystery which it signifies. Blessed virginity has recognised its author, and envying the integrity of the angels, consecrates itself to the bride-chamber of Him who is at once the bridegroom and the son of perpetual virginity."[11]

We have already seen that the state of perfection presupposes a special call from God. This is preeminently true of the specific wedlock with Christ which results from consecrated virginity. Here Jesus's secret call to the soul plays an even more central and more indispensable part. That call is not simply "follow me", but "Come, my beloved, and be wed. The winter is past, the voice of the turtle dove invites — the vines in flower give forth their fragrance." He alone can invite a soul to that marriage with Himself which, as a source of grace, infinitely exceeds every aid the soul can receive from other goods. If the pure man needs a special knowledge of God's approval before he lifts the veil in marriage from the mystery of sex, how much more will the soul require a direct call from Christ the heavenly bridegroom to enter into wedlock with Him and renounce forever the voluntary disclosure of that secret. So sublime is this state and so great its demands that no man could presume to choose it, unless by the invitation of Jesus Himself.

"When Thou didst look upon me Thine eyes impressed on
    me Thy grace.
For which Thou didst love me,
And by which mine eyes deserved to worship what they beheld
    in Thee."

ST. JOHN OF THE CROSS

11. Quoted from Fr. Athanasius Wintersig, op. cit.

Consecrated Virginity as a State of Love

ONCE AGAIN we must insist: The holiness of individuals gives God far greater glory than the state of consecrated virginity as such. Holiness is the one supreme goal common to all alike, by which we mean the real and complete transformation of a man in and by the power of Christ, the light and reflection of Jesus whose likeness shines out from us when "we no longer live, but Christ in us." Interior wedlock with Jesus, the highest measure of supernatural love for Him and for all creatures in Him, henceforward our life-principle, the undisputed sovereignty of that Divine Life imparted to us in baptism—these are the essential aims set before all men without exception, the mission of every human being, whose accomplishment gives God greater glory than any state of life, however exalted, or the act of heroism by which that state is chosen. "This is the will of God, your sanctification." For holiness alone is full membership in Christ's mystical body; the holier we are, the more does our entire personality share in the Divine Life of Christ and with and in Him glorify God.

However exalted the rank of consecrated virginity, what St. Paul says of the gift of prophecy and the faith which removes mountains is still applicable—the man who possesses it without love is nothing. Here, in fact, where the state as such is the external embodiment of the life which in the fullest measure is a life for Jesus, and as a marriage with Christ demands that supreme nuptial love, the object for which it was chosen is attained only if Christ's bride is distinguished among all others by her love for Him. Everything forces us to the conclusion that the moral significance and value of consecrated virginity, as opposed even to the most perfect purity, consists wholly in this wedlock with Christ, this mystery of supernatural love. The consecrated virgin is therefore a true bride of Christ, realizes what her exalted state of life objectively signifies, and *lives* as Christ's bride, only when her life represents a greater love than that demanded by the state of matrimony.[1]

It is easy to see why this point cannot be overemphasized. This sublime state of life, renouncing, as it does, the highest earthly partnership of love and necessarily demanding an unremitting watchfulness in all relations with others, especially with the opposite sex, involves the danger that the heart may grow hard and torpid, the soul be dulled and deadened.[2] Like the danger of relapsing into earthly passions, this peril also can be escaped only by the grace which flows from wedlock with Christ. Indeed, this hardening of the heart is as much an interior return to the world as the positive indulgence in earthly joys. Both alike are an infidelity to the heavenly bridegroom, a turning away from Him. For to His bride also Jesus says: "I came to cast fire upon the earth, and what will I but that it be kindled?"

A greater love, then, is what the life of Christ's bride must represent, a greater love of Jesus, the source of love, but also a greater share in Jesus's love for all creatures. The love of the consecrated virgin must embrace

---

1. "It is obvious, nevertheless, that states of life that in themselves open a freer and wider field to love are a standing witness to those who have chosen them that they have committed themselves unreservedly to love God in a higher measure and with a greater fervour than others." Charles Gay, op. cit.

2. This is the meaning of St. Augustine's warning (*Enarrationes in Psalm. 99*): "If they are virgins, of what use is integrity of the body, when the spirit has been corrupted? Better humble marriage than proud virginity."

creatures also, and not only her "neighbors" in general, but particular persons whom she must love in their concrete individuality. Nor need she love all men equally, for her Lord Himself wept over Lazarus's tomb and felt a special love for St. John and the Magdalene. Nor is there any limit to the *degree* and *depth* of love which Christ's bride may possess for *particular* creatures. It is only the *kind* of love that is restricted. She may love only in Jesus, with Jesus, and through Jesus. But for that very reason her love is far purer and deeper, as it is also *greater*, than all other — merely natural — love, because it is in a greater degree a participation in the love of Jesus, the God-man, for His creatures. It is this holy, yet entire personal love of individuals that we find in St. Bernard — himself an exemplar of the soul that is Christ's bride and the theologian of her nuptial love — when he writes in the following terms to Duchess Ermangard of Brittany: "Would that I could open out my soul to you, as I do this paper! Could you but read in my heart the love toward you which God's hand has written there. You would then understand that no tongue or pen could express what the spirit of God has impressed so intimately upon my soul. And though, indeed, I am now present with you in spirit, though absent in body, you cannot see me as I am. Yet there is a way by which if you cannot know my meaning in full you may conjecture something of it. Enter your heart and there behold mine, and attribute to me at least as much love for you as you feel in yourself for me.... You will now understand how you have kept me with you. I (to confess the truth) go nowhere away from you without you. ...I have received news that delights my heart, the news that you have found peace. I am delighted, because you inform me of your happiness, and the knowledge of your joy is medicine to my spirit."

The virgin's heart must be far more generous in its love than even the heart of the married; it must be inebriated by that supernatural love which destroys all selfishness, and must contain supereminently all genuine love and actual surrender to creatures. The closer a soul is united with God, Who is *Love*, the more it loves. Surely the bride of Christ, the Son of the Eternal Father, wedded as she is to Love incarnate, must exceed all in love. We know now why consecrated virginity represents the most exalted state on earth: because it is the objective embodiment of love's supreme mystery, so far as it is immediately communicable to a creature; because it involves a marriage in the strictest sense with Christ; and because it is not only the state of greatest purity, but the state of greatest love. The vocation of Christ's bride is simple—to love. St. Theresa of the Child Jesus discovered this secret; and what is perhaps the sublimest poem ever wrought by the spirit of man speaks as follows of His bride:

> "In the inner cellar of my beloved have I drunk, and when I came forth to wander o'er the wide plain I knew nothing, and lost the flock which before I had followed. There He gave me His caress, there He taught me secret wisdom of sweetest savour, there I gave myself to Him, wholly and without reserve, there I promised to be His bride. My soul is engaged and all that I have in His service; no longer do I keep a flock *nor follow any occupation: my sole business is love.* If henceforward you never see or meet me on the common pasture, you may say that I have lost myself, that walking the ways of God's love I have been lost and found." (St. John of the Cross, *Spiritual Canticle*)

This state of consecrated virginity is the highest because as a state of life it is the *expression* freely chosen as such of what is essentially the final and supreme vocation of every man.

Marriage and virginity now stand before the eyes of our mind with their profound intrinsic connection, both resplendent with purity, both a mystery of love. If our study of marriage proved that purity by no means implies any depreciation of sex, our study of virginity has penetrated its mystery more deeply still. The more fully a soul possesses the qualities of an earthly bride, the better fitted is it to become a bride of Christ.

But the virgins, like the martyrs, anticipate heaven, and take the kingdom of heaven by force: even on earth they can say: "Behold, what I longed for I already see; what I hoped for I already possess. I am espoused to Him whom the angels serve, at whose beauty sun and moon stand in amaze."

Index

CPSIA information can be obtained
at www.ICGtesting.com
Printed in the USA
FFOW02n2151051117
43306641-41873FF